Work
Your Way
Around
The World

Work
Your Way
Around
The World

A fresh and fully
up-to-date guide for
the modern working
traveller

Susan Griffith

10-07

22-

This edition published in Great Britain in 2007 by
Crimson Publishing
Westminster House
Kew Road
Richmond
Surrey
TW9 2ND

First published 1983
Revised every other year
Thirteenth edition 2007

A catalogue record for this book is available from the British library.

ISBN 978 1 85458 367 3

Printed and bound by MPG Books Limited, Cornwall

With thanks to Projects Abroad for the second image from bottom on the front cover.
All other cover illustrations © Getty images.

CONTENTS

WORK YOUR WAY

WORK YOUR WAY IN EUROPE

WORK YOUR WAY WORLDWIDE

ACKNOWLEDGMENTS

I never get tired of meeting and hearing from those intrepid travellers who are out there, sometimes living the life of Reilly, sometimes living on the edge. Their stories always enliven (and justify) my struggle to keep this book as up-to-date as possible. This new revised edition of *Work Your Way Around the World* would not have been possible without the help of hundreds of travellers who have generously shared their information over the years. Some have been writing to me over several editions, and their loyalty is greatly appreciated.

I would especially like to thank all those travellers who have crouched over keyboards in remote corners of the world and even (occasionally) bought a stamp to communicate with me since the last edition was prepared two years ago. All their pearls of travelling wisdom have been enthusiastically received and have been distilled into the pages that follow. My warmest thanks are owed to the following:

Jonathan Alderman, Peter Bainbridge, Justine Bakker, Jenna Bonistalli, Sophia Brown, Till Bruckner, Michael Buxton, Michael Cooley, Jessie Cox, Sitske De Groote, Louise FitzGerald, Stephanie Fuccio, Bradwell Jackson, Paul Jones, Ian Kent, Barry O'Leary, Kerian Parry, Sean Roberts, Emily Sloane, Jack Standbridge, 'Superbean', Joseph Tame, Danielle Thomas, Louis Tracy, Annelies van der Plas, Rebecca Wootten and Alicia Wszelaki.

While every effort has been made to ensure that the information contained in this book was accurate at the time of going to press, some details are bound to change within the lifetime of this edition. Wages, exchange rates and government policies are particularly susceptible to fluctuations, and the ones quoted here are intended merely as a guide.

If in the course of your travels you come across something which might be of interest to readers of the next edition, please write to Susan Griffith at Vacation Work/Crimson Publishing, Westminster House, Kew Road, Richmond, Surrey, TW9 2ND or email her at s.griffith@ntlworld.com (she promises to reply). This book depends very much on up-to-date reports from travellers who have worked their way. The best contributions will be rewarded with a free copy of the next edition or any other Vacation Work or Crimson title .

PREFACE

When I wrote the first edition of *Work Your Way Around the World* in the early 1980s, so few guidebooks about funding yourself on the road were available that travellers were grateful for any scrap of information and encouragement. Nowadays, working abroad has become such a mainstream idea that it has spawned thousands of websites, been featured on prime-time television and is serviced by a huge infrastructure for those who want to combine work and travel. Google has changed everything. The internet has become not just an asset but a necessity for the job-seeking traveller. To give just a couple of recent examples, all applications for New Zealand working holiday visas and for ancillary positions in Antarctica can be submitted only online.

But unless you know precisely what you are looking for on the internet, you can quickly (in fact within 0.19 seconds) become overwhelmed. You will feel as though you have been hit by a tsunami of undifferentiated information. Books are better at cutting through the clamour and rubbish, at creating order from the chaos. *Work Your Way* has grown up with the travel industry and takes account of all those shortcuts to fixing up work abroad that now exist. Among the many treasures on the internet is a recruitment website for Canadian ski resorts - www.wework2play.com – which could double as the motto of this book.

For this thirteenth edition of *Work Your Way Around the World* my network of informants has encompassed a traveller who got a job on a dude ranch in the American Rockies after cold-calling them out of the Yellow Pages, a newly graduated Canadian who spent a year teaching in Korea, a lively Flemish woman who volunteered at the Botanical Gardens in Berlin and interned with a consultancy company near Frankfurt, an American adventurer who at the time of writing had decided to stay awhile in Mauritania where he had talked an English language centre into giving him some hours of teaching, a serial volunteer in national parks in North America who especially enjoyed her stint at a school in the remote Canadian arctic, a young woman who spent her gap year (2006/7) picking grapes in France, joining a three-month conservation programme in South Africa and travelling in India, a long-time resident of Crete who reported on the temporary job opportunities on the island, an American photographer who fixes up short English teaching jobs – most recently in Poland and Taiwan – in order to extend her portfolio, a 19-year-old Australian who worked for a floatplane company in Vancouver before backpacking across Canada, and a round-the-world TEFLer who has picked up teaching jobs on arrival in Brazil, Ecuador, Thailand, Australia and this year Seville, Spain. Almost with one voice, they urge people whatever their backgrounds to give it a go and expose themselves to the unexpected friendliness and generosity of foreign residents and fellow travellers.

This past year saw the reprint of a book by Alistair Boyd about his 14-month round-the-world trip, after setting off in 1955 with only £5 in his pocket. Written when he was 23, *Royal Challenge Accepted* describes how he earned his way by teaching English, writing for newspapers, working his passage on freighters across the Atlantic and Pacific and hitching lifts on aeroplanes. When asked whether such a trip would be possible today, his answer was a regretful no. But modern adventurers and nomads are not so easily put off. Admittedly, a starting budget of £5 now would be cutting it a little too fine. And in today's world, the red tape is far harder to negotiate. All the more reason that today's travellers need this book, to advise on how to overcome the obstacles to picking up voluntary and paid jobs worldwide to fund further exciting travels.

Anybody who occasionally feels the call of the road, or the spirit of adventure flicker will, I hope, enjoy reading this book and dreaming. My aim has been to make the information in these 608 pages as concrete and up-to-the-minute as possible, to cut all the vague generalities and waffle. But among all the nearly 2,000 web addresses and realistic practical advice, the stories of working travellers are interwoven to inspire and encourage. As always, this book is intended to renew optimism and spark the imagination of all potential travellers.

Susan Griffith
Cambridge
May 2007

INTRODUCTION

LIVING THE DREAM

The idea of going all the way around the world holds more than a touch of romance. From the early heroic navigators like Ferdinand Magellan to the fictional traveller Phileas Fogg, circumnavigators of our planet have always captured the imagination of adventurous souls. More recently Michael Palin's globe-trotting television series attracted a huge audience, perhaps because so many of us relish a chance to imagine ourselves – impossibly ambitious as it sounds – as round-the-world explorers.

Nothing can compare with the joy of the open road. The sense of possibility and adventure brings feelings of exhilaration, long submerged in the workaday routines of home. Cheap air travel has opened up parts of the globe once reserved for the seriously affluent. When travelling in far-flung corners of the world, you can escape the demands of modern life in the Western world, the chores, the clutter, the technology. Whatever your stage of life, travelling spontaneously means you have the freedom to choose from an infinite spectrum of possibilities. Those who have experienced independent travel normally catch the bug and long to visit more places, see more wonders and spend a longer time abroad. Today trekking in the hinterland of Rio de Janeiro or diving in the Philippines can be within the grasp of ordinary folk. The longing might stem from a fascination left over from childhood with an exotic destination like Madagascar or Patagonia. The motivation might come from a friend's reminiscences or a television travelogue or a personal passion for a certain culture or natural habitat. At some point a vague idea begins to crystallise into an actual possibility.

That is the point at which the purple prose of brochure-speak must be interrupted by hard-headed planning. The first question is always: how can I afford such a trip? Magellan had the backing of the King and Queen of Spain, Phileas Fogg was a gentleman of independent means and Michael Palin could call on the resources of the BBC. How can ordinary people possibly move their dreams on to reality? The conventional means to an exciting end is to work and save hard. A grim spell of working overtime and denying yourself a social life is one route to being able to join a safari in Tanzania, a watersport instructor's course on the Mediterranean or a bungy-jump in New Zealand. But what if it were possible to skip this stage and head off towards the horizon sooner than that? Instead of trying to finance the expensive trips advertised in glossy travel brochures, what about try to find alternative ways of experiencing those same places at a fraction of the cost?

The catchy phrase 'work your way around the world' may contain the answer to the thorny question of funding. Picking up bits and pieces of work along the way can go a long way to reducing the cost. Even if it is unrealistic to expect to walk into highly paid jobs in Beijing or Berlin (though they do exist), other informal ways can be found of offsetting the cost of travel. Work-for-keep arrangements on a New Zealand farm or Costa Rican eco-lodge will mean that you have to save far less than if you booked a long-haul package holiday to those destinations – in some cases little more than the cost of the flight.

Short of emigrating or marrying a native, working abroad is an excellent way to experience a foreign culture from the inside. The plucky Briton who spends a few months on a Queensland cattle station will have a different tale to tell about Australia from the one who serves behind the bar in a Sydney pub. Yet both will experience the exhilaration of doing something completely unfamiliar in an alien setting.

Working abroad is one of the means by which it is possible to stay overseas for an extended period, to have a chance to get below the surface of a foreign culture, to meet foreign people on their own terms and to gain a better perspective on your own culture and habits. The traveller who spends a few weeks picking olives for a Cretan farmer will get a very different insight into the life and times of modern Greece from the traveller who looks after the children of a wealthy Athenian shipping magnate. And both will probably have more culturally worthwhile experiences than the traveller who is content with a fortnight in a party hostel on Corfu.

Anyone with a taste for adventure and a modicum of nerve has the potential for exploring far-flung corners of the globe on very little money. In an ideal world, it would be possible to register with an international employment agency and wait to be assigned to a glamorous job as an underwater model in the Caribbean, history co-ordinator for a European tour company or snowboard instructor in the Rockies. But jobs abroad, like jobs at home, must be ferreted out. The hundreds of pages that follow will help you to do just that.

THE DECISION TO GO

For many, deciding to get up and go is the biggest stumbling-block. Often the hardest step is fixing a departure date. Once you have bought a ticket, explained to your friends and family that you are off to see the world (they will either be envious or disapproving) and packed away your possessions, the rest seems to look after itself. Inevitably first-time travellers suffer some separation anxieties and pre-departure blues as they contemplate leaving behind the comfortable routines of home. But these are usually much worse in anticipation than in retrospect. As long as you have enough motivation, together with some money and a copy of this book, you are all set to have a great time abroad.

Either you follow your first impulse and opt for an immediate change of scenery, or you plan a job and a route in advance. On the one hand people use working as a means to an end; they work in order to fund further travelling. Other people look upon a job abroad as an end in itself, a way to explore other cultures, a means of satisfying their curiosity about whether there is any truth in the clichés about other nationalities. Often it is the best way to shake off the boredom which comes with routine. One contributor to this book felt quite liberated when she decided to drop everything – her 'cushy secretarial job, Debenhams account card, stiletto heels' – and embark on a working holiday around Europe. Another finally kicked over the traces of what he described as the 'Office Job from Hell' when he went off to Thailand to teach English.

When you are wondering whether you are the right sort to work abroad, do not imagine you are a special case. It is not only students, school-leavers and people on the dole who enjoy the chance to travel and work, but also a large number of people with a profession, craft or trade which they were happy to abandon temporarily. We have heard from a man who left the Met Office to pick grapes in Pauillac, a sixth-former teaching in Nepal, a mechanical engineer crewing on yachts in the South Pacific, an Israeli busker in Switzerland, a career civil servant who enjoyed washing dishes in a Munich restaurant, a physiotherapist who has packed cod in Iceland, a nurse who busked in Norway and another who has worked on a sheep station in Australia, an Australian teacher who became a nanny in Istanbul, a Scottish lawyer who worked as a chalet girl in a French ski resort, a German tourism trainee who planted trees in Canada, a chartered surveyor who took more than two years off from his job to work his way around the world and a journalist and tour operator couple who picked up casual jobs to fund their 'Stuff Mammon World Tour' and ended up living quite comfortably in Hong Kong. They were motivated not by a desire to earn money but by a craving for new and different experiences, and a conviction that not all events which make up one's life need to be career-furthering or 'success'-oriented.

PREPARATION

It is not the Mr. Micawbers of this world who succeed at getting jobs. (Mr. Micawber is the character in Charles Dickens's *David Copperfield* who is famous for living in hopeful expectation without taking any practical steps to bring about a successful outcome.) If you sit around as he did 'waiting for something to turn up' you will soon find yourself penniless with no prospects for replenishing your travel funds. If you wait in idleness at home or if you sit in your *pension* all day worrying about your dwindling euros or pesos, hesitating and dithering because you are convinced the situation is hopeless or that you lack the necessary documents to work, you will get absolutely nowhere.

Every successful venture combines periodic flights of fancy with methodical planning. The majority of us lack the courage (or the recklessness) just to get up and go. And any homework you do ahead of time will benefit you later, if only because it will give you more confidence. But it is important to strike a good balance between slavishly following a predetermined itinerary which might prevent you from grasping opportunities as they arise and setting off with no idea of what you're looking for. Many travel converts regret their initial decision to buy an air ticket with a fixed return date.

For many people, a shortage of money is the main obstacle. It is the rare individual who, like Ian McArthur, specialises in 'reckless arrivals' (Istanbul with £5, Cairo with $20 between him and a friend, New York with $1). Other people wait until they have substantial savings before they dare leave home which gives them the enviable freedom to work only when they want to.

SOMETIMES PENNILESSNESS ACTS AS A SPUR TO ACTION AS IT DID IN THE CASE OF ROGER BLAKE:

I left home with a substantial amount in savings. But they are long gone and for 18 months I have only been living off whatever I make locally. I have been down to just $50 more times than I'd care to remember. But somehow I always seem to come right. When I hear fellow travellers grumbling and sick with worry that they are down to $500, I cannot help but exclaim that they should enjoy it. In other words, when you've got it, flaunt it! Enjoy! There are those (usually with a few hundred dollars in the bank) who are 'looking for work' and those (including myself) who are looking for work. When your funds are REALLY low you WILL find a job, believe me.

Anyone embarking on an extended trip will have to have a certain amount of capital to buy tickets, visas, insurance (see below), etc. But it is amazing how a little can go a long way if you are willing to take a wide variety of casual jobs en route and willing to weather the financial doldrums. Stephen Psallidas had £40 one December and four months later (most of which was spent working as a waiter in Paris) he had £1,600 for a planned year in Australia.

MONEY

It is of course always a good idea to have an emergency fund in reserve if possible, or at least access to money from home should you run into difficulties (see section on 'Transferring Money' in *In Extremis* at the end of this book). Yet a surprising number of our correspondents have written in with the advice not to bother saving money before leaving home. Adrian McCay is just one who advocates packing your bags and going even if you have only £10 (though he later confesses that he left for Australia with £300). How much you decide to set aside before leaving will depend on whether or not you have a gambling streak. But even gamblers should take only sensible risks. If you don't have much cash, it's probably advisable to have a return ticket. For example, if you decide to crew on a yacht from the Mediterranean and don't have much money, you could buy a very cheap last minute return flight to Rhodes or the Canaries. If you succeed and waste the return half of your charter, wonderful; if not, you will have had a few weeks in the sun – disappointing perhaps but not desperate.

Attitudes to saving vary too. A Malaysian student, T. P. Lye, thinks that there is no better feeling than planning travels while saving for them (assuming you realise your ambition). On the other hand, Ian McArthur finds saving over a long period depressing and starts to long for those pints of lager and late-night curries of which he has been deprived. But even Ian admits that 'living on the edge' is no fun when only a couple of hundreds of unattainable pounds stand between you and the air ticket you want to buy. When Xuela Edwards returned after two years of working her way around Europe, she tried to hang on to the travelling mentality which makes it much easier to save money: *'My advice is to consider your home country in the same way as others. It makes you more resourceful. Try to avoid the car loans and high living that usually make up home life. I'm sure that the reason bulb workers in Holland for example save so much money is because they live in tents (which I admit would be tricky at home).'*

Mike Tunnicliffe spent more on his world travels than he intended but didn't regret it: *'Originally, I intended to finance my year with casual work and return to England having spent only the price of my ticket. In the end, I delved far deeper into my life's savings than I had intended to do, but I was fortunate in having savings on which to draw, and I made the conscious decision to enjoy my year while I had the chance. In other words, fun now, pay later!'*

Once you are resolved to travel, set a realistic target amount to save and then go for it wholeheartedly. Estimate how long it will take you to raise the desired amount and stick to the deadline as if your home country was going to sink into the ocean the day after. Don't get just any job, get one which is either highly paid (easier said than done of course) or one which offers as much overtime as you want. Dedicated working travellers consider a 70-hour week quite tolerable which will have the additional advantage of leaving you too tired to conduct an expensive social life. If you are already on the road and want to save, head for a place that allows this possibility, even if it won't be much fun. Adam Cook spent a miserable eight weeks picking peaches for an impossible French farmer but had saved £1,000 by the end of it. If you have collected some assets before setting off, you are luckier than most. Property owners can arrange for the rental money to follow them at regular intervals.

The average budget of a travelling student is about £20-£30 a day though many survive in some countries on half that. Whatever the size of your travelling fund, you should plan to access your money from three sources: cash, credit cards and travellers' cheques. Travellers' cheques are safer than cash, though they cost an extra 1% or 2%. They are a useful standby if you happen to find yourself stranded in a place without an ATM. American Express have monopolised the market and their cheques are sold by most banks plus Thomas Cook (who used to have their own brand). Try to avoid frequent transactions since suitable banks outside big cities are not always easy to find and encashing them can incur a service charge.

The most straightforward way to access money abroad is by using your bank debit card in hole-in-the-wall ATMs. There is usually a minimum fee for a withdrawal so you should get larger amounts out at one time than you would at home. Read the fine print on those boring leaflets that come with your debit card because it may be that your bank will gouge you with various loading fees, withdrawal fees and transaction fees. For example the transaction fee for withdrawing foreign currency abroad or paying at point-of-sale with a standard Maestro card is 2.65% in addition to the ordinary exchange rate disadvantage, plus cash machine withdrawals cost 2.25% of the sterling transaction up to a maximum of £4 (no minimum). The Point of Sale charge is a more reasonable 75 pence. If you are going to be abroad for a considerable period drawing on funds in your home account, it would be worth shopping around for the best deal which is at present offered in the UK by the Nationwide Building Society, whose FlexAccount debit card is the only one currently on the market that can be used abroad for free (www.nationwide. co.uk). The website www.moneyfacts.co.uk carries a comparative list of commission charged by the main providers (search for 'Travel Money').

American Express sells a Travellers Cheque Card which is a prepaid, reloadable card that can be used at ATMs and most shops but is not linked to your bank account. You must purchase the card (£20) and then load it up with a minimum of £200 in credit (or equivalent in Euros or dollars). It is a little like using a plastic card instead of travellers' cheques. Be aware that the exchange rate used for these card transactions is not at all favourable (typically 4% worse than the exchange rate used by American Express in other contexts). Similarly Visa's TravelMoney scheme available through Travelex (www.travelex.co.uk), which also operates like a phonecard that you top up with cash, charges steep exchange rates so it is probably preferable to rely on your ATM card. Note that an American Express card cannot be used to obtain cash in an emergency unless there is a local AmEx office.

It is advisable also to keep a small amount of cash handy. Euros are of course the currency of choice throughout Europe (including countries like Slovenia which have their own currency). Sterling is fine for many countries but US dollars are preferred in much of the world such as Latin America and Israel. The easiest way to look up the exchange rate of any world currency when planning your travels is to check on the internet (e.g. www.xe.net/ucc) or to look at the Monday edition of the *Financial Times*. Most banks require a few days' notice to obtain a foreign currency for you. Marks & Spencer's *Travel Money* offers favourable exchange rates with no commission or handling charges on currency or travellers' cheques. Furthermore these can be ordered online and posted to your home.

A credit card is useful for many purposes, provided you will not be tempted to abuse it. Few people think of crediting their Visa or Mastercard account before leaving and then withdrawing cash on the credit card without incurring interest charges (since the money is not being borrowed). Check the respective websites of your card issuer to see where your card is accepted abroad. A credit card can be invaluable in an emergency and handy for showing at borders where the officials frown on penniless tourists, as Roger Blake discovered when he tried to leave Australia on a one-way ticket:

> *On my world travels, I'm usually prepared to be challenged, by having printed bank statements (of borrowed money) at the ready. However, having never been asked before I didn't bother this time and, sods law, at Melbourne airport they weren't happy about allowing me to leave on a one-way ticket to New Zealand without proof of 'sufficient funds'. I pointed out that it states on my NZ work visa 'outward passage waived' but they were having none of it. I only had about A$400 in my pocket. But fortunately I have generous 'credit' available on my credit card. I was able to log onto my account via the internet and that was enough to persuade them to let me through...eventually, just one day short of a year to the day that I arrived.*

From London to La Paz there are crooks lurking, ready to pounce upon the unsuspecting traveller. Theft takes many forms, from the highly trained gangs of gypsy children who artfully pick pockets all over

Europe to violent attacks on the streets of American cities. Even more depressing is the theft which takes place by other travellers in youth hostels or on beaches. Risks can be reduced by carrying your wealth in several places including a comfortable money belt worn inside your clothing, steering clear of seedy or crowded areas, avoiding counting your money in public and moderating your intake of alcohol. If you are mugged, and have an insurance policy which covers cash, you must obtain a police report (often for a fee) to stand any chance of recouping part of your loss.

While you are busy saving money to reach your desired target, you should be thinking of other ways in which to prepare yourself, including health, what to take and which contacts and skills you might cultivate.

BAGGAGE

While aiming to travel as lightly as possible (leave the hair products behind) you should consider the advantage of taking certain extra pieces of equipment. For example, many working travellers consider the extra weight of a tent and sleeping bag worthwhile in view of the independence and flexibility it gives them if they are offered work by a farmer who cannot provide accommodation. A comfortable pair of shoes is essential, since a job hunt abroad often involves a lot of pavement pounding. Stephen Hands had his shoes stolen while swimming at night and found that bleeding feet were a serious impediment to finding (never mind, doing) a job.

Mobile phones are now *de rigeur* for any job hunt on the road (see section below on 'Keeping in Touch' for advice). Other items that can be packed that might be useful for a specific money-making project include a penny whistle or guitar for busking, a suit for getting work as an English teacher or data inputter, a pair of gloves (fingerless, rubber, as appropriate) for cold-weather fruit-picking, and so on. Leave at home anything of value (monetary or sentimental). The general rule is stick to the bare essentials (including a Swiss army knife – but not in your hand luggage if you're flying or it will be confiscated at security). One travelling tip is to carry dental floss, useful not only for your teeth but as strong twine for mending backpacks, hanging up laundry, etc. You might allow yourself the odd (lightweight) luxury, such as an iPod (though theft will be a worry and recharging a hassle), short-wave radio or a jar of peanut butter. If you have prearranged a job, you can always post some belongings on ahead.

Good maps and guides always enhance one's enjoyment of a trip. If you are going to be based in a major city, buy a map ahead of time. Plan to visit the famous map and travel shop Edward Stanford Ltd with branches in Bristol and Manchester as well as the mother-store in Covent Garden, London, whose searchable catalogue is now online at www.stanfords.co.uk. Also recommended is Daunt Books for Travellers (83 Marylebone High Street, London W1; 020-7224 2295) which stocks fiction and travel writing alongside guide books and maps. The Map Shop in Worcestershire (0800 085 4080/01684 593146; www.themapshop.co.uk) and Maps Worldwide in Wiltshire (01225 707004; www.mapsworld-wide.co.uk) both do an extensive mail order business in specialised maps and guide books.

Dozens of travel specialists throughout North America exist, including the Traveller's Bookstore (75 Rockefeller Plaza, 22 W 52nd; 212-664-0995) which sells guides, maps, travel-related books and products (free catalogue available). Also in Manhattan, The Complete Traveller Antiquarian Bookstore (199 Madison Ave, New York, NY 10016; 212-685-9007; www.completetravellerbooks.com) has a very knowledgeable staff and an impressive collection of antiquarian travel books. In Boston try the Globe Corner Bookstore in Harvard Square (www.globecorner.com) and in Canada, Wanderlust (1929 West 4th Avenue, Kitsilano, Vancouver, BC, V6J 1M7; 1-866 739 2182; www.wanderlustore.com).

Phrase books, dictionaries and teach-yourself language courses can be more useful once you arrive in a country than at home.

INSURANCE

Extensive information about health issues for travellers is given at the end of the next chapter about Travel. One of the keys to avoiding medical disaster is to have adequate insurance cover. All travellers must face the possibility of an accident befalling them abroad. In countries like India, Turkey and Venezuela, the rate of road traffic accidents can be as much as twenty times greater than in the UK. Research carried out by the Foreign & Commonwealth Office revealed that more than a quarter of travellers aged 16-34 do not purchase travel insurance, which means that about three million people are taking a serious risk.

Given the limitations of state-provided reciprocal health cover (i.e. that it covers only emergencies), you should certainly take out comprehensive private cover which will cover extras like loss of baggage and, more importantly, emergency repatriation. Every enterprise in the travel business is delighted to sell you insurance because of the commission earned. Shopping around can save you money. Ring several insurance companies with your specifications and compare prices. If you are going abroad to work, you are expected to inform your insurer ahead of time (which is often impossible). Many policies will be invalidated if you injure yourself at work, e.g. put out your back while picking plums or cut yourself in a restaurant kitchen, though it is not clear how they would know how or where the accident took place. If you snap your Achilles tendon, was it jumping off an orchard ladder or playing squash? There is no need to ask a broker to quote for a tailor-made policy since many of the backpacker policies specifically cover casual work.

Many companies charge less, though you will have to decide whether you are satisfied with their level of cover. Most offer a standard rate that covers medical emergencies and a premium rate that covers personal baggage, cancellation, etc. Some travel policies list as one of their exclusions: 'any claims which arise while the Insured is engaged in any manual employment'. If you are not planning to visit North America, the premiums will be much less expensive. Some companies to consider are listed here with an estimate of their premiums for 12 months of worldwide cover (including the USA). Expect to pay roughly £20-£25 per month for basic cover and £35-£40 for more extensive cover.

Club Direct, West Sussex (0800 083 2466; www.clubdirect.com). Work abroad is included provided it does not involve using heavy machinery; £310 for year-long cover including baggage cover; £220 for backpacker cover.

Columbus Direct, London EC2 (020-7375 0011; 08450 761030; www.columbusdirect.com). One of the giants in the field of travel insurance chosen by *Rough Guides* as their partner. From £280 for twelve months worldwide cover.

Coverworks/Visas-Australia, Cheshire (08702 862828). Policy specially designed for working holidays. In 2007 had a special offer of including a free working holiday visa for Australia with a 12-month worldwide policy costing £269 (€375).

Direct Line Insurance – 0845 246 8910; www.directline.com.

Downunder Worldwide Travel Insurance, London W2 (0800 393908; www.duinsure.com). Backpacker policy covers working holidays (excluding ladders and heavy machinery) starts at £250. Adventurer policy covering adventure sports costs £350.

Endsleigh Insurance – Offices in most university towns. 12 months of essential worldwide cover costs £287, £431 for comprehensive cover. Maximum age 35.

Europ-Assistance Ltd – 0870 737 5720; www.europ-assistance.co.uk. World's largest assistance organisation with a network of doctors, air ambulances, agents and vehicle rescue services managed by 208 offices worldwide. Voyager Travel policy covers periods from 6 to 18 months; sample price £580 for 12 months.

gosure.com – 0845 222 0020; www.gosure.com. Explorer one-year policies for 18-34 year olds cost £216 with no baggage cover, £240 with baggage cover.

MRL Insurance, Surrey (0870 876 7677; www.mrlinsurance.co.uk). £119 for 4 months, £219 for 12 months for under 35s.

Navigator Travel Insurance Services Ltd, Manchester (0161-973 6435; www.navigatortravel. co.uk).

Travel Insurance Agency, London N1 (020-8446 5414/5; www.travelinsurers.com). £275.

If you do have to make a claim, you may be unpleasantly surprised by the amount of the settlement eventually paid. Loss adjusters have ways of making calculations which prove that you are entitled to less than you think. For example when Caroline Langdon was mugged in Seville she suffered losses of about £100, for which her insurance company paid compensation of £22.30. The golden rule is to amass as much documentation as possible to support your application, most importantly a police report.

Recommended US insurers for extended stays abroad are International SOS Assistance Inc. (1-800-523-8930; www.internationalsos.com) which is used by the Peace Corps and is designed for people working in remote areas. A firm which specialises in providing insurance for Americans living overseas is Wallach & Company (1-800-237-6615; www.wallach.com).

SECURITY

Travel inevitably involves balancing risks and navigating through hazards real or imagined. The Foreign & Commonwealth Office of the UK government runs a regular and updated service; you can ring the Travel Advice Unit on 0870 606 0290 or check their website www.fco.gov.uk/travel. This site gives frequently updated and detailed risk assessments of any trouble spots, including civil unrest, terrorism and crime. Several years ago the FCO launched a 'Know Before You Go' campaign to raise awareness among backpackers and independent travellers of potential risks and dangers and how to guard against them, principally by taking out a water-tight insurance policy. The same emphasis can be detected on the FCO site launched in 2005: www.gogapyear.co.uk.

A couple of specialist organisations put on courses to prepare clients for potential dangers and problems on a world trip or gap year. Needless to say, these are normally aimed at naïve 18-year-olds whose parents are paying for the course, though they are open to anyone willing to pay the fee of £150-£350. The newest provider is Safetrek in Devon (01884 839704; www.safetrek.co.uk). Another training provider is Planet Wise near Oxford (0870 2000 220; www.PlanetWise.net) which runs one-day travel safety and awareness courses for £160.

QUALIFICATIONS

These sensible precautions of purchasing maps, buying insurance, finding out about malaria, etc., are relatively straightforward and easy. Other specific ways of preparing yourself, such as studying a language, learning to sail or dive, cook, drive or touch-type, or taking up a fitness programme, are a different kettle of fish. But the traveller who has a definite commitment may well consider embarking on a self-improvement scheme before setting off. Among the most useful qualifications you can acquire are a certificate in Teaching English as a Foreign Language (see chapter on *Teaching English*) and a knowledge of sailing or diving (see *Tourism* chapter for the address of a course which also offers job placement).

The person who has a definite job skill to offer increases his or her chances of success. After working his way from Paris to Cape Town via Queensland, Stephen Psallidas concluded '*There are several professions which are in demand anywhere in the world, and I would say that anyone who practises them would be laughing all the way to the 747. These are: secretary, cook/chef, accountant, nurse and hairdresser.*'

It is a good idea to take documentary evidence of any qualifications you have earned. Also take along a sheaf of references, both character and work-related, if possible, all on headed notepaper. It is difficult to arrange for these to be sent once you're on the road. An even smarter move is to scan these documents before you depart and email them to yourself. That way you can access them from any internet café around the world. It is a good idea to prepare your CV at the same time. When it comes time to apply for a job abroad, you'll have the template on the computer and can just tinker with it according to the vacancy you're going for.

LANGUAGE

Having even a limited knowledge of a foreign language is especially valuable for the jobseeker. Stephen Hands thinks that this can't be over-emphasised; after an unsuccessful attempt to find work in France, he returned to Britain and, even before phoning home, signed up for a language course (and received the additional perk of a student card).

Evening language classes offered by local authorities usually follow the academic year and are aimed at hobby learners. Intensive courses offered privately are much more expensive. If you are really dedicated, consider using a self-study programme with books and tapes (which start at £30), distance learning course or broadcast language course, though discipline is required to make progress. Although many people have been turning to the web to teach them a language, many conventional teach-yourself courses are still on the market, for example from OUP (www.askoxford.com/languages), Berlitz (020-7518 8300), the BBC (08700 100222), Linguaphone (0800 282417; www.linguaphone.co.uk) and Audioforum (www.audioforum.com). All offer deluxe courses with refinements such as interactive videos and of course these cost more. Linguaphone recommends half an hour of study a day for three months to master the basics of a language. Even if you don't make much headway with the course at home, take the tapes and books with you since you will have more incentive to learn once you are immersed in a language.

If you are interested in an obscure language and don't know where to study it, contact the National Centre for Languages (CILT, 020-7379 5101; www.cilt.org.uk) which has a certain amount of documentation on courses, especially in London.

A more enjoyable way of learning a language (and normally a more successful one) is by speaking it with the natives. The cheapest way to do this is to link up with a native speaker living in your local area, possibly by putting an ad in a local paper or making contact through a local English language school. Numerous organisations offer 'in-country' language courses, though these tend to be expensive. CESA Languages Abroad in Cornwall (01209 211800; www.cesalanguages.com) and Language Courses

Abroad Ltd (01509 211612; www.languagesabroad.co.uk) offer the chance to learn languages on location. Edinburgh-based Caledonia Languages Abroad (0131-621 7721; www.caledonialanguages.co.uk) offers language courses worldwide and in Latin America combines language courses with voluntary placements. In the USA, language learners might like to contact the National Registration Center for Study Abroad (www.nrcsa.com) for a listing of language schools in more than 39 countries. Many include options to participate in volunteer work or career-focused internships. An effective search engine for locating courses is provided by the Institute of International Education on www.iiepassport.org. Alternatives are www.abroadlanguages.com and www.worldwide.edu.

Another possibility is to forgo structured lessons and simply live with a family, which has the further advantage of allowing you to become known in a community which might lead to job openings later. Some tourist offices and private agencies arrange paying guest stays which are designed for people wishing to learn or improve language skills in the context of family life.

MAKING CONTACTS

> **BASED ON HIS YEARS OF LIVING ON THREE CONTINENTS, TILL BRUCKNER THINKS THAT LEARNING THE LANGUAGE IS PIVOTAL:**
>
> *Learning the local language will not only help you find a job on the spot, it also makes life abroad so much more rewarding. As an extra bonus, you'll find work easier to come by when you return home too. The first thing I do when I arrive somewhere now is to get myself language lessons. The teacher will have met many other foreigners, have local connections and speak some English. In other words, he or she is the natural starting point on your job hunt. If you make clear that you can only continue paying for your lessons if you find a way of earning some money, you've found a highly motivated ally in your search for work.*

The importance of knowing people, not necessarily in high places but on the spot, is stressed by many of our contributors. Some people are lucky enough to have family and friends scattered around the world in positions to offer advice or even employment. Others must create their own contacts by exploiting less obvious connections.

Dick Bird, who spent over a year travelling around South America, light-heartedly anticipates how this works:

> *In Bolivia we hope to start practising another survival technique known as 'having some addresses'. The procedure is quite simple. Before leaving one's country of origin, inform everyone you know from your immediate family to the most casual acquaintance, that you are about to leave for South America. With only a little cajoling they might volunteer the address of somebody they once met on the platform of Clapham Junction or some other tenuous connection who went out to South America to seek their fortunes. You then present your worthy self on the unsuspecting emigré's doorstep and announce that you have been in close and recent communication with their nearest and dearest. Although you won't necessarily be welcomed with open arms, the chances are they will be eager for your company and conversation. Furthermore these contacts are often useful for finding work: doing odd jobs, farming, tutoring people they know, etc.*

Everyone has ways of developing links with people abroad. Think of distant cousins and family friends, foreign students met in your home town, pen friends, people in the town twinned with yours, etc. Maybe you dimly recall that someone you went to school with moved to Hong Kong or Tenerife and you could have a go at tracing them through the friendsreunited website. Human rights groups in your home country might have links with your destination or even know about opportunities for doing voluntary work in their offices abroad. Jacqueline Edwards placed a small notice in European vegetarian newsletters asking for a live-in position for herself and her young son.

School exchanges and or staying in youth hostels can result in valuable contacts. To join the YHA in the UK, visit your nearest hostel or contact the HQ in Derbyshire (0870 770 8868; www.yha.org.uk). Annual membership for the under-26s costs £9.95.

One way of developing contacts is to join a travel club such as the Globetrotters Club (BCM/Roving, London WC1N 3XX; info@globetrotters.co.uk) for £15/€27 a year. The Club has no office and so correspondence addressed to the above box office address is answered by volunteers. Members receive a bi-monthly travel newsletter and a list of members, many of whom are willing to extend hospitality to other globetrotters and possibly to advise them on local employment prospects.

Servas International is an organisation begun by an American Quaker, which runs a worldwide programme of free hospitality exchanges for travellers, to further world peace and understanding. Normally you don't stay with one host for more than a couple of days. To become a Servas traveller or host in the UK, contact Servas Britain (020-8444 7778; www.servasbritain.u-net.com) who can forward your enquiry to your Area Co-ordinator. Before a traveller can be given a list of hosts (which are drawn up every autumn), he or she must pay a fee of £25 (£35 for couples) and be interviewed by a co-ordinator. Servas US is at 11 John St, Suite 505, New York, NY 10038 (212-267-0252; www.usservas.org). There is a joining fee of US$85 and a refundable deposit of $25 for host lists in up to five countries.

Hospitality exchange organisations can make travel both interesting and cheap. Bradwell Jackson had been mulling over the possibility of travelling the world for about a decade before he finally gave up his drug abuse counselling job in the US to take off for an indeterminate period of time. On his earlier travels he had discovered the benefits of joining Servas and two other hospitality exchange programmes Global Freeloaders (www.globalfreeloaders.com) and the Hospitality Club (www.hospitalityclub.org) which has a special area for hitch-hikers. His first destination was Mexico where to his delight he found English teaching work at the first place he happened to enquire in Mexico City:

> *I really must say right away that Servas is not simply for freeloading in people's homes. However, once you take the plunge and commit to wandering the earth, things just start to fall into place. If you belong to clubs such as Global Freeloaders, Hospitality Club, or any of the other homestay organisations, don´t be surprised if the family you stay with invites you for an extended stay. The first such family I stayed with in Mexico invited me to stay for six months. All they asked is that I help with the costs of the food they prepared for me and hot water I used.*

When you register with the Hospitality Club, Global Freeloaders, place2stay.net or the Couchsurfing Project (www.couchsurfing.com), all of which are completely free, you agree to host the occasional visitor in your home in order to earn the right to stay with other members worldwide. Another possibility is the Hospitality Exchange based in Montana (hospitalityex@yahoo.com; www.hospex.net) which charges $20 for a year's membership.

Other hospitality clubs and exchanges are worth investigating. Women Welcome Women World Wide (tel/fax 01494 465441; www.womenwelcomewomen.org.uk) enables women of different countries to visit one another. There is no set subscription, but the minimum donation requested is £25/$45, which covers the cost of the membership list and three newsletters in which members may publish announcements. There are currently 2,500 members (aged 16-80+) in 70 countries.

The internet has of course revolutionised the way in which networks of contacts and friends can be developed. Catharine Carfoot spent a year after university in Australia and New Zealand:

> *I thought you might be interested in the extent to which my adventures in cyber space have impacted on my real life exploits. For example the only genuine residents I met while travelling in the South Island (apart from people running hostels, which hardly counts) were either people I met on the net or their friends. It would make my mother's hair curl to say the least of it, but I stayed with a very nice chap (father of two) in Rotorua who took me out on his boat as well as making me dinner and letting me sleep in his spare room. Obviously one has to counsel caution in these matters but equally trust is a two-way street.*

TRAVELLING ALONE

Many travellers emphasise the benefits of travelling alone, especially the chance to make friends with the locals more easily. Most are surprised that loneliness is hardly an issue, since there is always congenial company to be met in travellers' hostels, harbourside pubs, kibbutzim, etc., some of whom even team up with each other if they happen to be heading the same direction. Of course, if you are working in a remote rural area and don't speak the language fluently, you will inevitably miss having a companion and may steer away from this kind of situation if it bothers you. If you are anxious about the trials and traumas of being on your own, try a short trip and see how you like it.

Women can travel solo just as enjoyably as men, as Woden Teachout discovered when she was 24:

> *I'm female, American and like to travel alone. I have travelled with friends on occasion which is definitely more 'fun' but it lacks the perilous sense of possibility and adventure that I love most about travelling. Whatever situations you get yourself into when you are on your own, you have to get out of. I have been terribly frightened: I spent the night of my 21st birthday huddled in a cellar hole in downtown Malmo, Sweden, wet and shivering, knowing that a local rapist had claimed three victims within the fortnight. But by the same token, the glorious moments, the stick-out-your-thumb-and-be-glad-for-whatever-is-going-to-happen-next moments, the feelings of triumph and absolute freedom, are uniquely yours.*

TRAVELLING COMPANIONS

You have to be fairly lucky to have a friend who is both willing and available when you are to embark on a working trip. If you don't have a suitable companion and are convinced you need one, you can search on appropriate internet forums like Lonely Planet's thorntree, www.backpackers.com with its 'Travel Buddies' forum, www.companions2travel.co.uk or (if appropriate) www.gapyear.com, any of which might turn up a like-minded companion. Start your search for a companion well in advance of your proposed departure date so there will be a chance to get to know the person a bit before the trip.

There are also a few agencies in the US which try to match up compatible travel companions for an annual or a one-off fee, for example TravelChums (www.travelchums.com). Sarah Clifford describes the easiest way of all to find companions: *'I think you should warn people that* Work You Way Around the World *is infectious. Even people who I would never have thought would want to go anywhere start flicking through the pages, then get more and more absorbed, become incredibly enthusiastic and demand to go with me on my travels!'*

STAYING IN TOUCH

Fixing yourself up with a web-based e-mail account before leaving home is now virtually compulsory. This allows you to keep in touch with and receive messages from home and also with friends met on the road. The most heavily subscribed service for travellers is still Hotmail (www.hotmail.com or www. hotmail.co.uk) though its popularity occasionally places strains on the system. A popular alternative, also free, is provided by Yahoo (http://mail.yahoo.com) with which British users can register for a yahoo. co.uk address.

Roaming charges for mobiles can cost an arm and a leg. Contact your mobile phone company to check on coverage; if not you may need to take it into a shop to have the phone 'unlocked'. Also check what deals your provider offers. In 2006, O_2 got a lot of publicity for cutting costs for travellers with its 'My Europe' package and a newer 'Chosen Country' deal. Vodafone's 'Passport' is a free tariff option available with any handset, which allows you to make calls at your home tariff after paying a 75p connection fee. It is available in most of Europe, Australia, New Zealand and Japan but not North America (www.vodafone.co.uk/passport).

Warn friends not to call your UK mobile while you are away; you will be paying for all incoming calls from abroad. If you are staying in one country for more than a few weeks and use your phone a lot, consider getting either a cheap local mobile phone or a local Sim card for your UK mobile, not forgetting to inform the folks back home of the new number. Local texts and calls tend to be very cheap and incoming calls from abroad are free, which avoids the massive charges when using your UK mobile.

Even better, ensure your UK contacts have the special access codes available for low cost dialling to your destination. One of the most often recommended discount companies (for people phoning abroad from the UK) is www.telediscount.co.uk in the UK which offers unbeatable prices: in many cases you can make an international call at local rates.

A plethora of companies in the UK and US sell pre-paid calling cards intended to simplify international phoning. You credit your card account with an amount of your choice (normally starting at £10 or £20), or buy a card for $10 or $20. You are given an access code which can be used from any phone. Lonely Planet, the travel publisher, has an easy-to-use communications card called eKit which offers low cost calls, voice mail and email (www.lonelyplanet.ekit.com). A company called 0044 (www.0044.co.uk) sells foreign Sim cards which allow you to take your mobile with you and call at local rates while you're away. For example the price of a Sim card for Spain (with up to €22 credit and free Nokia unlocking) costs £30. A global Sim card might be the answer; for example GoSim costs £35 or you can compare other brands at onecompare.com.

The technically minded might wish to take a digital camera in order to be able to send photos home electronically or set up their own website or blog (i.e. web log) to share their travel tales with family and friends. Lots of companies will help you create your own blog, for example www.blogger.com/start (which is free) while http://community.webshots.com is designed for people to upload their photos (also free for storing up to 240 photos). Another recommended site for starting your own blog or following the travel blogs of others is http://blogs.bootsnall.com.

Clearly there are advantages to such easy communication, though there are also travellers out there who spend an inordinate amount of time tracking down and inhabiting cybercafés instead of looking around the country and meeting locals in the old-fashioned, strike-up-a-conversation way. Danny Jacobson from Madison is also ambivalent about its virtues (and committed his thoughts to paper): *'I've met loads of travellers using e-mail to meet people online, to keep in touch with people they've met travelling, to find out information about a place and to publish their own adventures. It all seems to be making the world an incredibly small place. Myself, I admit I've spent a fair share of money on e-mail and rely on it at times quite a bit. I worry that it is getting easier and easier to do everything from a sitting position.'*

It would be a shame if e-mail deprived long-term travellers of arriving at a *poste restante* address and having the pleasure (sweeter because it has been deferred) of reading their mail.

RED TAPE

PASSPORTS AND WORK VISAS

A ten-year UK passport costs £66, and should be processed by the Identity & Passport Service within three weeks. The one-week fast track application procedures costs £91 and an existing passport can be renewed in person at a passport office but only if you have made a prior appointment by ringing the Passport Adviceline on 0870 521 0410 and are willing to pay £108. Passport office addresses are listed on passport application forms available from main post offices. All relevant information can be found on the website www.passport.gov.uk.

Most countries will want to see that your passport has at least 90 days to run beyond your proposed stay. If your passport is lost or stolen while travelling, contact first the police then your nearest Consulate. Obtaining replacement travel documents is easier if you have a record of the passport number and its date and place of issue, so keep these in a separate place, preferably a photocopy of the title page.

The free reciprocity of labour within the European Union means that the red tape has been simplified (though not done away with completely). See the chapter *EU Employment*. As will become clear as you read further in this book, work permits/work visas outside the EU are not readily available to ordinary mortals. In almost all cases, you must find an employer willing to apply to the immigration authorities on your behalf months in advance of the job's starting date, while you are in your home country. This is usually a next-to-impossible feat unless you are a high-ranking nuclear physicist, a foreign correspondent or are participating in an organised exchange programme where the red tape is taken care of by your sponsoring organisation. Wherever possible, we have mentioned such possibilities throughout this book. The official visa information should be requested from the Embassy or Consulate (if only to be ignored); addresses in London and Washington are listed in Appendix 4. For general information about visas, see the next chapter.

Once you are installed in a country, be aware that any enemy you make who knows that your legal position is dodgy will be tempted to tip off the authorities. For example if you are trying to freelance as a guide and are resented by local operators, you may find yourself in trouble.

STUDENT CARDS

With an International Student Identity Card (ISIC; www.isiccard.com) it is often possible to obtain reduced fares on trains, planes and buses, £1 off each night's stay at a youth hostel, discounted admission to museums and theatres, and other perks. The ISIC is available to all students in full-time education. There is no age limit though some flight carriers do not apply discounts for students over 31. To obtain a card (which is valid for 15 months from September) you will need to complete the ISIC application form, provide a passport photo, proof of full-time student status (NUS card or official letter) and the fee of £7.

Take these to any students' union, local student travel office or send a cheque for £7.50 to ISIC Mail Order, DPS Hull Ltd, Unit 132, Lois Perlman Centre, Goulden St, Hull HU3 4DL. When issued with an ISIC, students also receive a handbook containing travel tips, details of national and international discounts and how to get in touch with the ISIC helpline, a special service for travelling students who need advice in an emergency.

If you are not eligible, people have been known to walk into their local college, say that they are about to start a course and request a student card. There are a great many forgeries in circulation, most of which originate in Bangkok, Istanbul or Cairo. Simon Calder, travel editor of the *Independent* and no longer in the first flush of youth, picked up a student card for £3 on Bangkok's Khao San Road just before Christmas 2006.

BUREAUCRACY AT LARGE

Having your papers in order is a recurring problem for the working traveller. Andrew Winwood thinks that this book underestimates the difficulties: *'I wish that you would be honest about immigration, obtaining the proper visas, etc. But having said that, I wouldn't have had the nerve to go in the first place if I'd known how hard it would be.'*

It is easy to understand why every country in the world has immigration policies which are principally job protection schemes for their own nationals. Nevertheless it can be frustrating to encounter bureaucratic hassles if you merely intend to teach English for a month or so, and there is really no local candidate available with your advantages (e.g. fluency). In all the countries with which we deal, we have tried to set out as clearly as possible the official position regarding visas and work and/or residence permits for both EU and non-EU readers.

If you are cautious by nature you may be very reluctant to transgress the regulations. People in this category will feel much happier if they can arrange things through official channels, such as approved exchange organisations or agencies which arrange permits for you, or by finding an employer willing to get them a work permit, which must normally be collected outside the country of employment. Arranging things this way will require extra reserves of patience.

It seems that a great many decisions are taken at the discretion (or whim) of the individual bureaucrat. Whether or not a document is issued seems to depend more on the mood of the official than on the rulebook. Leeson Clifton from Canada followed all the rules for getting official status as a temporary employee in Norway. When she took her passport to the police for their stamp she was told it would take two weeks and she could not work in the meantime. She returned to the same office the next day and got it done on the spot. She concludes: *'The left hand didn't know what the right hand was doing, but of course this is the same in any country. When dealing with government authorities always be patient and pleasant, but keep on asking for what you want and in most cases you'll get it (eventually). Losing your cool gets you nowhere; after all they have no obligations to you.'*

Other travellers are prepared to throw caution to the winds and echo Helen Welch's view that *'government bureaucracy is the same anywhere, i.e. notoriously slow; by the time the system discovers that you are an alien you can be long gone.'* This is more serious in some countries and in certain circumstances than in others, and we have tried to give some idea in this book of the enthusiasm with which the immigration laws are enforced from country to country and the probable outcome for employer and employee if the rules are broken. The authorities will usually turn a blind eye in areas where there is a labour shortage and enforce the letter of the law when there is a glut of unemployed foreign workers. If you do land an unofficial job (helping a Greek islander build a taverna, picking kiwifruit in New Zealand, doing odd jobs at an orphanage in central Africa) try to be as discreet as possible. Noisy boasting has been the downfall of many a traveller who has attracted unwelcome attention. It is always important to be as sensitive as possible to local customs and expectations.

Another veteran traveller is suspicious of the value of using official channels: *'One of my conclusions is that going through the official channels and taking advice from officialdom is often a mistake. 'Officially' (i.e. the view of the British Council in Paris) it is very hard to get teaching work, as there are so many highly qualified English people living in Paris. The French agricultural information office warns that there is very little in the way of farm work for foreigners.'*

And yet he had a variety of teaching and agricultural jobs throughout France. He claims that if he had believed all that he had been told by officialdom and had taken all the suggested precautions, he would never have been able to go in the first place.

GETTING A JOB BEFORE YOU GO

The subsequent chapters contain a great deal of advice and a number of useful web addresses and phone numbers for people wishing to fix up a job before they leave home. If you have ever worked for a firm with branches abroad (e.g. Virgin Records, Starbucks, Kelly Girl, even McDonald's) it may be worth contacting sister branches abroad about prospects. There is a lot to recommend prior planning especially to people who have never travelled abroad and who feel some trepidation at the prospect. There are lots of 'easy' ways to break into the world of working travellers, for instance working on an American summer camp, joining a two-week voluntary workcamp on the continent or going on a kibbutz, all of which can be fixed up beforehand. Inevitably these will introduce you to an international circle of travellers whose experiences will entertain, instruct and inspire the novice traveller.

Professional or skilled people have a chance of prearranging a job. For example nurses, plumbers, architects, motor mechanics, piano tuners, teachers, divers, hairdressers, secretaries and computer programmers can sometimes find work abroad within their profession by answering adverts in British newspapers and specialist journals, by writing direct to hospitals, schools and businesses abroad, and by registering with the appropriate professional association.

But the majority of people who dream about working their way around the world do not have a professional or trade qualification. Many will be students who are on the way to becoming qualified, but are impatient to broaden their horizons before graduation. The main requirement seems to be perseverance. Dennis Bricault sent off 137 letters in order to fix up a summer job as a volunteer at an alpine youth hostel.

ROB ABBLETT RECOUNTS HOW DOGGEDNESS WORKED IN HIS FAVOUR:
Armed with a couple of addresses of Corsican clementine farmers, I hounded them mercilessly over the years with my requests for work. The organic fruit farm wouldn't employ me on any terms and seemed a bit miffed when I phoned them. My present employer would throw my letters straight into the wastepaper basket. By pure chance one of them escaped his attention and got through to the sleeping partner who happened to have had an English nanny and spoke excellent English. He persuaded my boss to employ me on condition that he accepted full responsibility for kicking me off the orchard if I turned out to be like the last Brit that worked here many years ago. Apparently I have been an exemplary worker and have been wined and dined over the Christmas period with many a banquet.

Several editions ago, a reader and traveller (Stephen Hands) expressed his longing for a miraculous network of information for working travellers:

Wouldn't it be great if someone set up a scheme, whereby people could forward correspondence to an exchange of some kind, for people to swap addresses of places they've worked abroad. For example someone planning to work in Nice could write to some agency to obtain the address of another travel-ler who could tell him what the manager's like or if the chef is an axe-wielding homicidal maniac or that the accommodation is a hole in the bottom of the local coal mine. This would enable working travellers to avoid the rip-off places; also it might save them turning up in places where the work potential is zero.

The scheme which Stephen thought was a pipedream just a few years ago now has a name, the internet. Somewhere on the web, you can probably find out that the axe-wielding chef has been replaced by a Quaker and that the coal mine has been tastefully refurbished.

EMPLOYMENT AGENCIES

Adverts that offer glamorous jobs and high wages abroad should be treated with scepticism. They are often placed by one-man companies who are in fact selling printed bumph about jobs on cruise ships, in the United States or wherever, which will not get you much closer to any dream job whatever their ads promise (e.g. 'Earn up to £400 a week in Japan' or 'Would you like to work on a luxury cruise ship?'). A not infrequent con is to charge people for regular job listings and contacts in their chosen destination, which may consist of adverts lifted from newspapers or addresses from the *Yellow Pages* long out of date.

By law UK employment agencies (and those in many other countries) are not permitted to charge jobseekers an upfront fee. They make their money from the company or organisation seeking staff. Every so often a bogus agency will place false recruitment advertisements in the tabloid press charging a 'registration fee' or a compulsory charge for extra services. They then disappear without trace. Some operate as clubs offering members certain services such as translating and circulating CVs. Before join-ing any such club, try to find out what their success rate is. You could even ask to be put in touch with someone whose membership resulted in their getting a job.

There are of course reputable international recruitment agencies in Britain, the USA and elsewhere, many of them operating solely online. Specialist agencies for qualified personnel can be very useful, for example agencies for financial and IT vacancies with branches worldwide. Agencies with a range of specialities from disc jockeys for international hotels to English teachers for language schools abroad are mentioned in the relevant chapters which follow.

Do not neglect EURES, the state-run employment service within Europe (see chapter on *EU Employ-ment*), which has been successfully helping unskilled workers to find seasonal jobs in other member states, as well as assisting professional jobseekers.

INTERNATIONAL PLACEMENT ORGANISATIONS

Established organisations that assist students and other young people to work abroad are invaluable for guiding people through the red tape problems and for providing a soft landing for first time travellers:

BUNAC, 16 Bowling Green Lane, London EC1R 0QH (020-7251 3472; www.bunac.org) is a student club (annual membership £5) which helps students and in some programmes non-students to work abroad. It has a choice of programmes in the United States, Canada, Australia, New Zealand, South Africa, Ghana, Costa Rica, Peru, Cambodia and the newest programme, Teach & Travel China. Programme fees usually include an arrival orientation course, UK and in-country support, accommodation and food. BUNAC USA (PO Box 430, Southbury, CT 06488; 203-264-0901) runs outgoing programmes for Americans to the UK, Ireland and many other countries.

Global Choices, Barkat House, 116-118 Finchley Road, London NW3 5HT (020-7433 2501; info@globalchoices.co.uk). Voluntary work, internships, practical training and work experience worldwide from 2 weeks to 18 months. Placements are arranged for a fee in many fields in Australia, USA, Ireland, Argentina, Brazil, Spain, Greece, China and India.

IST Plus Ltd, Rosedale House, Rosedale Road, Richmond, Surrey TW9 2SZ (020-8939 9057; info@istplus.com; www.istplus.com). Partner agency of the Council for International Educational Exchange in the US. Working programmes for Britons in the USA, Australia, New Zealand, Thailand and China. Americans who want to join a teaching programme in Chile, China, Spain or Thailand should contact CIEE, 7 Custom House Street, 3rd Floor, Portland, ME 04101; 207-553-7600; www.ciee.org/teach.aspx.

Real Gap, First Floor, No 1 Meadow Road, Tunbridge Wells, Kent TN1 2YG (0870 803 1570; www.realgap.co.uk). Gap year and work abroad programmes in Australia, New Zealand, Canada and the USA plus volunteer programmes in Africa and Asia.

Working Abroad/InterExchange Inc, 161 Sixth Avenue, New York, NY 10013 (212-924-0446; www. workingabroad.org). Various work, au pairing and volunteer programmes in the UK, Australia, Spain, France, Germany, Italy, Mexico, Costa Rica, Peru, Kenya, South Africa, Namibia and India.

Overseas Visitors Club South Africa, Cape Town (0861 682 682; www.ovc.co.za) can organise work placements in the UK, USA, Ireland and Canada, and book Kibbutz volunteer placements in Israel through one of 20 OVC offices throughout South Africa.

CCUSA, 1st Floor North, Devon House, 171/177 Great Portland St, London W1W 5PQ (020-7637 0779; www.ccusa.com). Offices also in Leeds and Musselburgh in the UK and in Sausalito California. Work Experience programmes in the US (general and summer camps), in Australia/New Zealand and Brazil plus summer camp counselling in Canada, Russia and Croatia, and teaching in China.

Twin Work & Volunteer Abroad, 67-71 Lewisham High Street, London, SE13 5JX (0800 804 8380 or 020-8297 3251; workabroad@twinuk.com; www.workandvolunteer.com). Work experience in Europe and volunteer programmes in three continents.

Youth exchange organisations and commercial agencies offer packages which help their nationals to take advantage of the work permit rules. For example Travel CUTS in Canada operate the SWAP programme (www.swap.ca) which sends Canadian students to work in the UK, Ireland, France, Austria, Germany, Australia, New Zealand, South Africa, Brazil, China and Japan. Rita Hoek is one person who decided to participate in an organised programme, the Work & Travel Australia programme offered by Travel Active based in Venray, Netherlands:

> *Though I'm not suggesting these programmes are perfect for everybody's specific plans, it's been of great help to me. You join a discount-group airfare (cheaper and easier), they help with getting a visa and most programmes provide a first week of accommodation, assistance in getting a tax file number and opening a bank account, a service to forward your mail, general information about work and travelling and heaps more. If you don't want to feel completely lost at the airport while travelling for the first time (as I was), I can surely recommend it.*

IAESTE is the abbreviation for the International Association for the Exchange of Students for Technical Experience. It provides international course-related vacation training for thousands of university-level students in 80 member countries. Placements are available in engineering, science, agriculture, architecture and related fields. British undergraduates should apply directly to IAESTE UK at the British

Council (www.iaeste.org.uk). The US affiliate is the Association for International Practical Training or AIPT (410-997-3069; www.aipt.org or www.iaesteunitedstates.org,) which can make long and short-term placements of graduates and young professionals as well as college students in related fields.

In the US, several agencies offer a range of programmes for varying fees. The *Alliance Abroad Group* (www.allianceabroad.com) arranges a variety of overseas placements including work placements in the UK, France and Australia, teaching in Spain, China and Argentina, and volunteer placements in Ecuador, Costa Rica, Brazil and Peru.

USEFUL SOURCES OF INFORMATION

Websites and reference books, directories of jobs and specialist journals can all be useful. Publications covering specific countries or specific kinds of work (e.g. *Teaching English Abroad* or *Living, Studying and Working in Italy* are mentioned in the relevant chapters. Of general interest are:

The Directory of Summer Jobs Abroad (Vacation Work, Westminster House, Kew Road, Richmond TW9 2nd; www.vacationwork.co.uk; £10.99 plus £1.75 postage). Published each November.

Taking a Gap Year (Vacation Work, 5th edition 2007; £12.95) by me. Covers all the specialist placement organisations with first-hand accounts, as well as extensive country-by-country advice on how to wing it on your year off.

Prospects - www.prospects.ac.uk. Official UK graduates' career websites, Links to 'Jobs Abroad'.

Transitions Abroad, PO Box 745, Bennington, VT 05201; 802-442-4827; (www.transitionsabroad.com). Annual magazine subscription (six issues) costs $28 within the US, $46 abroad. Website is a superb resource for work abroad, study abroad, cultural travel overseas and international living.

A host of commercial websites promises to provide free online recruitment services for travellers. These include the admirable Jobs Abroad Bulletin (www.jobsabroadbulletin.co.uk), a free monthly e-bulletin on working abroad and gap years, www.seasonworkers.com, www.natives.co.uk (originally for ski resort work but has now branched out), www.anyworkanywhere.com, www.jobsmonkey.com (especially for North America), http://jobs.escapeartist.com, www.hotrecruit.co.uk, and so on. Everywhere you look on the internet potentially useful links can be found. Nextstep (www.nextstepuk.co.uk) is aiming to establish itself as the UK's working holiday and backpacker travel community and classifieds. Travel Tree (www.traveltree.co.uk) is a directory aimed at people looking for educational travel, gap year ideas, internships, volunteering, etc. JobSlave.com was launched in 2006 as a network of recruitment sites aimed at the youth market covering everything from bar jobs in Sydney to banking jobs in London. It comprises findaGapjob.com, findaStudentjob.com, findaGraduatejob.com and findaSkiResortjob.com. A surprising number of company home pages feature an icon you can click to find out about jobs; often to be found under the heading 'About Us'. Elsewhere on the web, committed individuals around the world manage non-commercial sites on everything from kibbutzim to bar-tending.

ADVERTISEMENTS

If you are thinking of advertising your interest in working abroad, try to be as specific as possible. While surfing the net you will often come across postings along the lines of 'Looking for no-skills job anywhere. Please help me' which seems worse than hopeless. For a good example of a reader not targeting his self-advertisement carefully enough, see Fergus Cooney's story in the chapter on *Teaching English*.

An increasing number of foreign newspapers can be read online making it much easier to reply to job advertisements as soon as they appear than in the old days when you had to track down a hard copy in a library or embassy reading room. Nevertheless any potential employer is likely to look askance at someone in Dudley or Kirkcaldy who answers an ad for someone to start immediately in a pub on Corfu or a fruit farm in Western Australia.

Web forums can be goldmines. Annelies Van der Plas has used the Dutch travellers' forum www. wereldwijzer.nl to good effect more than once. The advert she placed was very general:

> *Instead of waiting and looking on www.wereldwijzer.nl, we placed an advertisement there ourselves. I was enthusiastic about this forum, because I had got my job on the Greek island of Kos this way. The advertisement was something like this: 'Two hard-working students are looking for a job abroad for July and August'. Our first response was from a man from a campsite where they all walk naked (don't know the English word for it). As you can imagine we waited for other responses. The second response was from a Dutch woman also from a campsite in France. The job was to entertain the children on the campsite and help the owners with cleaning, preparing the barbecue and serving dinner. At first we were a little sceptical, but we looked at their homepage and searched for information and experiences about the campsite. Our contact (Jane) told us that it's not really a party job, but instead you would be part of 'the family'. By this she meant that people at the campsite eat (almost) every night on one long table together. You really get to know the people. This is the thing that persuaded us to take the job. Another plus was that Jane gave us the e-mail address of a girl who worked there before. She told us what we could expect, which was helpful. Within one or two weeks we received our train tickets in the post (worth about €200 each). Also I received a phone call from Jane; we talked about some practical things and fun stuff, like horse riding (she was very glad that for the first time one of her employees liked horses). The best thing to do before you accept a job abroad is to search the internet for experiences, which is what we did.*

One of the most useful sites is the free community noticeboard Craigslist which started in San Francisco in 1995 but has spread to 450 cities from Auckland to Buenos Aires, Moscow to Cairo. With notification of about half a million new job ads a month, it is probably the biggest job board in the world, as well as carrying accommodation listings and everything else. It also lists many unpaid jobs and internships.

Unless you have very specialised skills, it is probably not worth paying for an advert in a foreign newspaper since anyone interested in hiring you would probably want to meet you first. For certain categories, it might be worth checking *LOOT* which bills itself as 'London's noticeboard' (www.loot.com). Among its many categories of classified ads (which are free to private advertisers) are 'International Jobs Offered/ Wanted' (which doesn't usually contain anything very exciting) and 'Au Pair Jobs Offered/Wanted.'

GETTING A JOB ON ARRIVAL

For those who leave home without something fixed up, a lot of initiative will be needed. Many travellers find it easier to locate casual work in country areas rather than cities, and outside the student holiday periods (although just before Christmas is a good time, when staff turnover is high). But it is possible in cities too, on building sites, in restaurants and in factories. If you go for the jobs which are least appealing, e.g. an orderly in a hospital for the criminally insane, a loo attendant, doing a street promotion dressed as a koala or a hamburger, a pylon painter, assistant in a battery chicken farm, salesman of encyclopaedia, dog meat factory worker, or just plain dogsbodies, the chances are you will be taken on sooner rather than later.

It always helps to have a neat appearance in order to dissociate yourself from the image of the hobo or hippy. You must show a keenness and persistence which may be out of character but are often essential. Even if a prospective employer turns you down at first, ask again since it is human nature to want to reward keenness and he or she may decide that an extra staff member could be useful after all. Polite pestering pays off. For example, if your requests for work down on the docks produce nothing one day, you must return the next day. After a week your face will be familiar and your eagerness and availability known to potential employers. If nothing seems to be materialising, volunteer to help mend nets (thereby adding a new skill to the ones you can offer) and if an opening does eventually arise, you will be the obvious choice. If you want a job teaching English in a school but there appear to be no openings, volunteer to assist with a class one day a week for no pay and if you prove yourself competent, you will have an excellent chance of filling any vacancy which does occur. So patience and persistence should become your watchwords, and before long you will belong to the fraternity of experienced, worldly-wise travellers who can maintain themselves on the road for extended periods.

Casual work by its very nature is changeable and unpredictable and can best be searched out on the spot. It pays to have your wits about you at all times. According to a collection of the oddest odd jobs spotted on the Lonely Planet website, a penniless traveller in Paris was nearly killed by a bag of tools falling from a construction site. He caught the bag, climbed the scaffolding with the tools, told the builders how they could easily arrange a pulley and was immediately hired as a mason's assistant for a month.

Despite her tender years when she first started travelling and fending for herself, Carisa Fey had learned the value of quiet observation: *'My motto was and still is watch the people that do the job you want and then copy them. So my first few days in London I spent walking through the city watching people. After I found out what the businesswomen wore, I went to the shops and bought as cheaply as possible a very neat suit and the right kinds of accessories.'*

You may follow the advice in this book to go to Avignon, France in August, for example, to pick plums or to resorts along the Ocean Road in Australia to get bar work. When you arrive you may be disappointed to learn that the harvest was unusually early or the resort has already hired enough staff. But your informant may go on to say that if you wait two weeks you can pick grapes or if you travel to the next reef island, there is a shortage of dining room staff. In other words, one thing leads to another once you are on the track.

A certain amount of bravado is a good, even a necessary, thing. If you must exaggerate the amount of experience you have had or the time you intend to stay in order to get a chance to do a job, then so be it. There is little room for shyness and self-effacement in the enterprise of working your way around the world. (On the other hand, bluffing is not recommended if it might result in danger, for example if you pretend to have more sailing experience than you really do for a transatlantic crossing.)

AFTER CIRCUMNAVIGATING THE GLOBE AND WORKING IN A NUMBER OF COUNTRIES DAVID COOKSLEY COMMENTS:
All the information and contacts in the world are absolutely useless unless you make a personal approach to the particular situation. You must be resourceful and never retiring. If I were the manager of a large company which needed self-motivating sales people, I'd hire all the contributors to Work Your Way Around the World *since they have the ability to communicate with anyone anywhere in any language.*

HostelBookers.com offers independent travellers:
→ Budget Accommodation in Over 2,000 Destinations
→ No Booking Fees
→ Customer Ratings & Recommendations
→ Worldwide News, Travel & Events

hostelbookers.com
Great Hostels. Free Booking. No Worries.

MEETING PEOPLE

The most worthwhile source of information is without question your fellow travellers. After you have hurled yourself into the fray you will soon become connected up with kindred spirits more experienced at the game than you, whose advice you should heed. Other travellers are surprisingly generous with their information and assistance. David Hewitt claims that this cannot be overemphasised; he and his Brazilian wife have been consistently helped by their compatriots from Berlin to Miami. A Mexican correspondent who arrived in Toronto cold sought out the Latino community and, after taking their advice, was soon comfortably housed and employed.

If you arrive in a new place without a prearranged contact, there are many ways of meeting the locals and other travellers to find out about job possibilities. Backpacker hostels are universally recommended, especially out of season, and many hostel wardens will be well versed in the local opportunities for casual jobs. Of course hostels are also the best places for working travellers to stay. Bookings at hostels worldwide can be made free of charge on www.hostelbookers.com whose website contains useful travel tips on topics such as taking a laptop on your travels. Check the websites www.hostels.com, www.hostels.net or www.hostelworld. com for a selection worldwide. The VIP Backpackers hostel group includes hundreds of hostels in Australia, New Zealand, South Africa and Europe; a membership card costs £16.50 (www.vipbackpackers.com).

Universities and polytechnics are good meeting places in term-time and also during the vacations when it is often possible to arrange cheap accommodation in student residences. Seek out the overseas student club to meet interesting people who are foreigners just like you. Investigate the student or bohemian parts of town where the itinerant community tends to congregate. Go to the pubs and cafés frequented by worldly-wise travellers (often the ones serving Guinness).

If you have a particular hobby or interest, ask if there is a local club, where you will meet like-minded people; join local ramblers, cyclists, cavers, environmental activists, train spotters, jazz buffs – the more obscure the more welcome you are likely to be. Join evening language courses, frequent the English language bookshop (which may well have a useful notice board) or visit the functions of the English language church, where you are likely to meet the expatriate community or be offered free advice by the vicar. Marta Eleniak introduced herself to the local Polish club, since she has a Polish surname and a fondness for the country, to ask if she could put up a notice asking for accommodation.

The kindly soul to whom she was speaking told her not to worry about it; she'd find her something she could move into the next day. She has come to the conclusion that learning to be a 'fog-horn' is an invaluable characteristic.

TILL BRUCKNER HAS (RELUCTANTLY) BEEN PERSUADED THAT HOBNOBBING WITH THE RICH AND POWERFUL CAN BE THE KEY TO JOB SUCCESS:
The one lesson I have failed to learn over and over again is the value of socialising. In Bolivia, I shoved a pamphlet advertising myself as a trekking guide under the doors of dozens of agencies without ever getting a reply. It just doesn't work that way. Nobody will ever bother to ring you if they don't know you. A week before I left, I met an old Bolivian friend and when I told him that I'd been unable to find work, he said he couldn't believe it because his cousin had an agency and needed a German speaker. In the Sudan, I sent off my CV to all major NGOs offering myself as an unpaid volunteer. All I got was two negative replies. A week before I left (again) I went to a social event at a foreign embassy where I got talking with the head of a big charity. She told me about the problems they had with writing endless reports. I asked her why she hadn't replied to my application and it turned out she'd never seen it. The moral of the story is that in some countries the best place to start looking for a job is down the pub, especially the sort of pub where well-off locals and expats hang out. I absolutely loathe exactly that kind of establishment but you might well hit the jackpot in there. You're unlikely to get hired by someone poor after all.

Not that the people you will meet in this way will necessarily be able to give you a full-time job, but it sets the wheels in motion and before too long you will be earning your way by following their advice and leads. Provided your new friends speak the local language better than you, they can make telephone calls for you, translate newspaper advertisements, write out a message for you to show possible employers and even act as interpreters. One young Englishman was dragged along to the local radio station by his Italian hosts who persuaded the station to have him co-host an afternoon programme. The manager of another traveller's hostel in Cairo wrote out an Arabic notice for him, offering private English lessons.

If your contacts can't offer you a real job they might know of a 'pseudo job' or 'non-job' which can keep you afloat: guarding their yacht, doing odd jobs around their property, babysitting, typing, teaching the children English, or just staying for free. These neatly avoid the issue of work permits, too, since they are arranged on an entirely unofficial and personal basis. Human contacts are usually stronger than red tape.

CHANCE

When you first set off, the possibility of being a sheep-catcher in the Australian outback or an English tutor in Turkey may never have crossed your mind. Chance is a fine thing and is one of the traveller's greatest allies. Brigitte Albrech had saved up leave from her job in the German tourist industry to go on holiday in Mexico. While there, she became friendly with some Québecois who invited her to join them as tree planters in Western Canada, and she never made it back to her job.

There will be times when you will be amazed by the lucky chain of events which led you into a certain situation. 'Being in the right place at the right time' would have made a suitable subtitle to this book, though of course there are steps you can take to put yourself in the right place, and this book tries to point out what these might be. Here are some examples of how luck, often in combination with initiative, has resulted in travellers finding paid work:

- Mark Kilburn took up busking in a small Dutch town and was eventually asked to play a few nights a week in a nearby pub for a fee.
- Stuart Britton was befriended by a fisherman in a dusty little town in Mexico and was soon tutoring some of the fisherman's friends and acquaintances (and living in his house).
- While standing in a post office queue in the south of France, Brian Williams overheard the word *boulot* (which he knew to mean odd job) and cerises. He tapped the lady on the shoulder and offered his cherry picking expertise. After a protracted search for the address she had given him, he finally asked directions of someone who offered him a job in their orchard instead.
- On a flight to Reykjavik, Caroline Nicholls happened to sit next to the wife of the managing director of a large fish-packing cooperative in Iceland who told her they were short of staff.
- After finishing his summer stint as a camp counsellor in the US, Mark Kinder decided to try one parachute jump. He enjoyed it so much that he learned how to pack parachutes and was able to fund himself at the aerodrome for months afterwards.
- While looking for work on a boat in Antibes, Tom Morton found a job as a goatherd for six weeks in the mountains near Monte Carlo.
- Dominic Fitzgibbon mentioned to his landlady in Rome that he intended to leave soon for Greece since he had been unable to find a job locally in six weeks of looking. She decided he was far too nice to become a washer-up in a taverna and arranged for him to work as a hall porter at a friend's hotel.
- A. Gowing was a little startled to wake up one evening in Frankfurt station to find a middle-aged woman staring down at him. She offered him the chance of working with her travelling fun-fair.
- While getting her jabs for Africa at a clinic in Gibraltar, Mary Hall (a nurse cycling across Europe) noticed a door marked 'District Nurses', barged in and the following week had moved in as a live-in private nurse for a failing old lady.
- While shopping in a supermarket in Cyprus, Rhona Stannage noticed a local man with a trolley full of wine and beer, and assumed it could not be for his own consumption. She approached him, ascertained that he ran a restaurant and a day or two later was employed as a waitress.
- Connie Paraskeva shared a taxi in Bangkok with an American nurse who told her about a vacancy in a refugee camp.
- While sunbathing on an isolated Greek beach, Edward Peters was approached by a farmer and asked to pick his oranges.

The examples could be multiplied *ad infinitum* of how travellers, by keeping their ears open and by making their willingness to help obvious, have fallen into work. One of the keys to success is total flexibility. Within ten minutes of a chance conversation with a family sharing her breakfast table in an

Amsterdam hotel, Caroline Langdon had paid her bill, packed her bags and was off to Portugal with them as their mother's help.

Of course there is always such a thing as bad luck too. You may have received all sorts of inside information about a job on a Greek island, a vineyard or in a ski resort. But if a terrorist attack has decimated tourism (as happened in Bali bombings in 2002) or if there was a late frost which killed off the grapes or if the snowfalls are late arriving for the ski season (as in 2006/7), there will be far fewer jobs and your information may prove useless. Unpredictability is built into the kinds of jobs which travellers do.

DESIGN

But you cannot rely on luck alone; you will have to create your own luck at times. You may have to spend many hours surfing the internet, or apply to 20 hotels before one will accept you or you may have to inform 20 acquaintances of your general plans before one gives you the address of a useful contact.

You must check notice boards and newspaper advertisements, register with agencies and most important of all use the unselective 'walk-in-and-ask' method, just like jobseekers anywhere. The most important tools for an on-the-spot job hunt are a copy of the *Yellow Pages* and a phone. When Mary Hall was starting her job search in Switzerland, a friend gave her an odd piece of advice which she claims works, to smile while speaking on the phone. Some people say that all initial approaches are best made by telephone since refusals are less demoralising than in person and you need not worry about the scruffiness of your wardrobe.

One old hand Alan Corrie, describes his approach: *'The town of Annecy in the French Alps looked great so I found a fairly cheap hostel and got down to getting organised. This meant I was doing the rounds of the agencies, employment office, notice boards and cafés for a few days. After a matter of minutes in a town, I begin to sprout plastic bags full of maps, plans, lists, addresses and scraps of advice from people I have met on the road.'* Alan sounds unusually cheerful and optimistic about job-hunting and the result is that he worked in Europe for the better part of a decade. He concludes *'Looking for work in Annecy was an enjoyable pastime in early autumn. Making contacts and job hunting in a new place is a whole lot more fun than actually working and worrying about the bills as I've often found before'.*

Our working wanderers have displayed remarkable initiative and found their jobs in a great variety of ways:

■ Waiter in Northern Cyprus: I arranged my job by writing direct to the restaurant after seeing a two-minute clip on a BBC travel programme. Rita wrote back and offered me a job.

■ Farmhand on a Danish farm: I placed an advert in *Landsbladet,* the farmers' magazine, and chose one from four replies.

■ Au pair to a family in Helsinki: I found work as a nanny in Finland simply by placing advertisement cards in a few playgroups.

■ Teacher at a language school in southern Italy: We used the *Yellow Pages* in a Sicilian Post Office and from our 30 speculative applications received four job offers without so much as an interview.

■ Winery guide in Spain: I composed a modest and polite letter and sent it to an address copied from one of my father's wine labels. I was astonished at their favourable reply. Several years later the same contributor wrote to say: *'I sent a copy of the page in your book where I am mentioned to prospective employers in Australia, and I was offered a job on a vineyard near Melbourne.'*

■ Factory assistant in Ghana: I asked the local Amnesty International representative for any leads.

Implicit in all these stories is that you must take positive action.

REWARDS AND RISKS

THE DELIGHTS

The rewards of travelling are mostly self-evident: the interesting characters and lifestyles you are sure to meet, the wealth of anecdotes you will collect with which you can regale your grandchildren and photos with which you can bore your friends, a feeling of achievement, an increased self-reliance and maturity, learning to budget, a better perspective on your own country and your own habits, a good sun tan... the list could continue. Stephen Psallidas summed up his views on travelling: *'Meeting people from all over the world gives you a more tolerant attitude to other nationalities, races, etc. More importantly you learn to tolerate yourself, to learn more about your strengths and weaknesses. While we're on the clichés, you definitely 'find yourself, man'.'*

One traveller came back from a stint of working on the continent feeling a part of Europe rather than just an Englishman. (Perhaps some Brussels bureaucrat should be subsidising this book.) Sometimes travels abroad change the direction of your life. After working his way around the world in many low-paid and exploitative jobs, Ken Smith decided to specialise in studying employment law. After deciding to cycle through Africa on an extended holiday, Mary Hall ended up working for aid organisations in Africa and the Middle East.

One of the best aspects of the travelling life is that you are a free and unfettered agent. Albert Schweizer might have been thinking of the working traveller instead of equatorial Africans when he wrote: *'He works well under certain circumstances so long as the circumstances require it. He is not idle, but he is a free man, hence he is always a casual worker.'*

THE DANGERS

Of course things can go desperately wrong. As the number of young people backpacking to remote corners whether on gap years or otherwise has risen, it is inevitable that accidents will occur and will be widely reported. So if a young man slips down a waterfall in Costa Rica or a British girl is killed by a freak accident with a high voltage cable in Ecuador or a bus carrying overlanding travellers is held up by armed bandits in the Andes, the world hears about it. On the other hand if a student dies of a drug overdose or is killed on his bicycle in his hometown, this is not reported nationally.

A much less remote possibility than murder or kidnapping is that you might be robbed or lose your luggage or become involved in a traffic accident. You may get sick or lonely, or fed up, have a demoralising run of bad luck or fail to find a job, and begin to run out of money (if this is the case, consult the chapter *In Extremis*).

Many unofficial jobs carry with them an element of insecurity. You may not be protected by employment legislation and may not be in a position to negotiate with the boss. Often the work may be available to travellers like you because the conditions are unacceptable to a stable local population (or because the place is too remote to have a local population). Phil New is probably right when he says that the travellers who worry that they won't get paid or won't get hired are the very ones who do encounter problems. If you have cultivated the right attitude, you will not hesitate to drift on to a new situation if the old one should become undesirable for any reason.

Exploitative working conditions will show you how much you are prepared to tolerate. Paul Bridgland was not sorry to have worked for a tyrannical and abusive boss in Crete, since he now thinks he has developed such a thick skin that no future employer could penetrate it.

Much is now said about 'socially responsible tourism' and perhaps working travellers who put up with dreadful employers are doing both their host community and other travellers a disservice. Stephen Psallidas's advice (based on his own experience of exploitative Greek bosses) is not to put up with it: *'My advice when you are mistreated or your employer acts unprofessionally is to shout back when they shout at you. If things don't improve threaten to walk out and then do so. You will be doing a favour to future working travellers, and you will almost certainly be able to find something else if you try hard enough.'*

Charlotte Jakobson's worst employer was a hotelier in the middle of nowhere in Norway. When she discovered how underpaid she was she contacted a union official who was shocked and wanted to take action. Today she regrets that she was so keen to get away that she didn't stay to present the case and thinks of other girls who were probably subjected to the same bad experiences as a result.

Some people set off with false expectations about the life of the working traveller. Armin Birrer (who has travelled long enough to have earned his right to make such pronouncements) says that some of the enthusiasm with which travel writers tend to glorify travel should be moderated a little. The travelling life is full of uncertainty and hardship. To quote the inveterate working traveller Stephen Psallidas once more, *'I would say that the bad times even outnumber the good times, but the good times are great and the bad times are good for you in the end.'*

Even when a planned working holiday does not work out successfully, the experience will be far more memorable than just staying at home. This view is held by Stephen Hands who didn't regret his decision to go abroad to look for work (although it didn't work out) but he did regret boasting to all his friends that he was off for an indefinite period to see the world. After writing pages about her dodgy and difficult jobs in Australia, Emma Dunnage concluded with a typical paradox: *'But we did have the best time of our lives.'*

Though travelling itself is never dull, a job which you find to help out your finances along the way may well be. True 'working holidays' are rare: one example is to exchange your labour for a free trip with an outback Australian camping tour operator (see *Australia* chapter). But in many cases, the expression 'working holiday' is an oxymoron (like 'cruel kindness'). Jobs are jobs wherever you do them. David Anderson, who found himself working on an isolated Danish farm where he didn't feel at home in any way, recommends taking (a) your time to decide to accept a job, (b) a copy of *War and Peace* and (c) enough money to facilitate leaving if necessary. The best policy is to leave home only after you have the reserves to be able to work when you want to.

> **ONE OF THE UNEXPECTED DRAWBACKS OF BECOMING A GLOBAL CITIZEN WAS IDENTIFIED BY CARISA FEY:**
> *One of the blessings and the curses of travelling a lot is that your best friends live all over the world. Good, because you always have an excuse to go and visit a foreign country. But bad because you usually never have more than one close friend nearby.*

COMING HOME

Kristin Moen thinks that there should be a big warning at the beginning of *Work Your Way Around the World*: WHEN YOU FIRST START TO TRAVEL THERE IS NO WAY YOU CAN STOP! Correspondents have variously called travel an illness and an addiction. Once you set off you will probably come across a few restless souls for whom the idea of settling down is anathema and for whom the word 'vagabondage' was invented. One contributor met a 44-year-old New Zealander in Sydney who had been travelling and working for 25 years. Undoubtedly some use it as a form of escapism, believing it to be a panacea for all their problems. But these are the exceptions.

In the majority of cases, homesickness eventually sets in, and the longing for a pint of bitter, a bacon sandwich, a baseball game, Radio 4's 'Today' programme, green fields, Marks & Spencer or Mum's home cooking will get the better of you. Or perhaps duty intervenes as in the case of Michael Tunison: *'I had planned to go on to South America this summer, but I had to return home under emergency circum- stances. Not one, but two of my best friends were getting married. What is a poor globetrotter to do with people rather inconsiderately going on with their lives when he isn't even there? But after a year it was actually quite nice to have a chance to organise my things and repack for further adventures.'*

At some point your instinct will tell you that the time has come to hang up your rucksack (assuming you haven't sold it). After many years on the road Rob Abblett took stock: *'I decided to come back to England from Uruguay earlier than planned. I'd been robbed in Paraguay, got scared in Buenos Aires and decided that eight years of working around the world has been fantastic and worthwhile. But now I need to do something different.'*

Settling back will be difficult, especially if you have not been able to set aside some money for 'The Return'. As soon as he left Asia en route back from Australia, Riwan Hafiz began to feel depressed and when he arrived at Heathrow wanted to put a blanket over his head. It can be a wretched feeling after some glorious adventures to find yourself with nothing to start over on. One travel writer has compared the post Travel Blues to SAD (Seasonal Affective Disorder). Life at home may seem dull and routine at first, while the outlook of your friends and family can strike you as narrow and limited. If you have been round the world between school and further study, you may find it difficult to bridge the gulf between you and your stay-at-home peers who may feel a little threatened or belittled by your experiences. If you have spent time in developing countries the reverse culture shock may be acute, as Chris Miksovsky from Colorado discovered:

Memories of the trip already come racing back at the oddest of times. A few days after returning to the US, I went to a large grocery store with my mother. It was overwhelming. Rows and rows of colours and logos all screaming to get your attention. I wandered over to the popcorn display and stood dumbfounded by the variety: buttered, lite, generic, Redenbacker, Paul Newman's au naturel, from single serving sachet through economy family popcorn-orgy size. I counted over 25 unique offerings... of popcorn.

But it passes. The reverse culture shock normally wears off soon enough and you will begin to feel reintegrated in your course or job. In some cases the changes which travel have brought about may be more than just psychological; for example David Hewitt set off on his travels a bachelor, married a fellow volunteer from Brazil met on his kibbutz and then had a child whom they were trying to make into a working traveller before she reached her first birthday by putting her forward for promotions in the US.

People often wonder whether a long spell of travelling or living abroad will damage their future job prospects. According to numerous surveys on graduate employment, most employers are sympathetic to people who defer entry to the labour market. In the majority of cases, travel seems to be considered an advantage, something that makes you stand out from the crowd. Marcus Scrace found that even in his profession of chartered surveying, employers looked favourably on someone who had had the get-up-and-go to work his way around the world. Jeremy Pack chose to join the computing industry upon his return and claimed that he did not meet one negative reaction to his two years off. Naturally it helps if you can present your experiences positively, if only to prevent the potential employer from imagining you out of your skull on a beach in Goa for 12 months. Your travels must be presented constructively and not as an extended doss. Stephen Psallidas, who returned after three years on the road, is convinced that he would never have got a good job (as Projects Manager in Computer Education) before he left. Not that he gained any relevant experience on his travels but he had learned how to be persistent and pester employers for an interview.

Some hostility is probably inevitable especially when the job market is shrinking, making employers more conservative. Jane Thomas knew that it would be tough finding a job when she got back to England, but she didn't know how tough. Some interviewers did express their concern and suspicion that she would want to take off again (which at that time was exactly what she did want to do). But she also found that she could adapt the short-term jobs she had done in the US and Australia to fit whatever job she was trying to get. And after a certain period of time has elapsed, your absence from the conventional working world ceases to be an issue. At last report Jane had a job making videos with the possibility of some work with the BBC.

In some cases the jobs you have found abroad are a positive boost to your 'real life' prospects, as in the case of Michael Tunison from Michigan:

> *Newspaper work was exactly what I thought I was leaving behind by globetrotting. I'd temporarily sacrificed (I believed) my career as a journalist. The last place I thought I'd be working was at a daily in Mexico. But things never work out as planned and before I knew it I was the managing editor's assistant and a month or so later the managing editor of the paper's weekend editions. How ironic. By taking a step my newspaper friends believed to be an irresponsible career move, I was soon years ahead of where I'd have been following the old safe route back home.*

CONCLUSION

While some identify the initial decision to go abroad as the hardest part, others find the inevitable troughs (such as finding yourself alone in a sleazy hotel room on your birthday, running out of money with no immediate prospect of work, etc.) more difficult to cope with. But if travelling requires a much greater investment of energy than staying at home, it will reward the effort many times over.

A HOST OF TRAVELLERS HAVE MENTIONED HOW MUCH THEY VALUE THEIR COLLECTION OF MEMORIES. SINCE WE HAVE BEEN GUIDED BY THE EXPERIENCES OF ORDINARY TRAVELLERS THROUGHOUT THE WRITING OF THIS BOOK, LET ONE OF THEIR NUMBER, STEVE HENDRY, END THE INTRODUCTION:

I left home with about £100 and no return ticket. I spent two years in Israel, three years in Thailand, one year in Japan. I have lived in the sun for years, with Arabs on the seashore and with wealthy Japanese. If I can do it, you can too. I've learned so very much. Travelling is 100% fun and educational. What are you waiting for?

TRAVEL

Unscripted travel provides a chance to shed the clutter and flee the routines of modern student or worka-day life, to indulge in the unalloyed pleasure of choosing one or more destinations from among an infinite number of possibilities. The travel shelves of bookshops are dense with names to conjure with: Karako-ram, Kilimanjaro, Kalimantan, Bali, Cali and Mali. And of course Paris, Prague and Pennsylvania are not to be sniffed at either. Some people take time out to embark on a particular journey they have long dreamed of, to set off on journeys that range from straightforward backpacking to expeditions to organised adven-ture trips. The choices can be overwhelming: will it be trekking in the hinterland of Rio de Janeiro or finding the perfect beach on a Thai island? Attending one of the annual travel shows can help to formulate plans: the *Daily Telegraph's* Adventure Travel Show is in January each year, the *Times's* Destinations Show is in February, One Life Live in March and the Great Escape exhibition in Dublin is in April.

Canvassing the options for exciting travel at bargain prices is an endlessly fascinating pastime. Just in the week that this is being written, a one-way fare from Gatwick to Hong Kong was available for £109 (including taxes) and a return fare from Manchester to Cuba was £99 before tax. The price of flying has fallen substantially in real terms over the past two decades and it is quite possible that we are currently experiencing the heyday of flying. Fares will gradually creep up as anxiety about environmental degrada-tion takes hold and governments begin to impose higher taxes and more restrictions. The increase of Air Passenger Duty in the UK from February 2007 from £20 to £40 on longhaul flights and £5 to £10 on European flights is indicative. As inveterate traveller Dave Sands (whose moniker is 'the professional traveller') wrote in 2007: *'Of course don't ignore another compelling reason for travelling NOW: the pos-sibility that the government may make it too expensive in the future with so called green taxes.'*

There follow some general guidelines for finding bargains in train, coach, ship and air travel. More detailed information on specific destinations can be found in travel guides from Lonely Planet and Rough Guides. The amount of travel information on the internet is staggering and this chapter cannot hope to tap its resources. There are websites on everything from sleeping in airports (www.sleepinginairports.net) to sharing lifts across North America (www.erideshare.com). Many sites have pages of intriguing links; to name just two, try www.bugeurope.com ('BUG' stands for Backpackers' Ultimate Guide) and www.budgettravel.com.

AIR

Scheduled airfares are best avoided. They are primarily designed for airline accountants and business-men on expense accounts. You should be looking at no-frills ticketless flying, cheap charters and last minute discounted tickets. Air travel within individual countries and continents is not always subject to this choice, though some special deals are available.

For longhaul flights, especially to Asia, Australasia and most recently Latin America, discounted tickets are available in plenty. Previously the sale of these tickets was restricted to the original 'bucket shops', often seedy discount agencies. Now high street travel agents such as Trailfinders and Flight Centre and hundreds of travel websites are competing to offer the lowest fares. Because of their enormous turnover and sophisticated computer systems, they can often offer the best deals.

The very lowest fares are still found by doing some careful shopping around well in advance. Last minute reductions are rare nowadays since airlines operate on the no-frills airline principle of charging more the later you book. Check adverts in the travel press like the Saturday *Independent* and in the London free magazine *TNT*. Phone a few outfits to find the baseline fare and then try to find better on the internet. A good start when browsing the internet is www. www.flightfind.co.uk or www.cheapflights. co.uk. The monolithic sites like www.opodo.com, www.travelocity.com, www.expedia.co.uk and www. lastminute.com which also owns www.flights4less.co.uk are worth checking but do not always come up with the best deals. When users log onto their destination, they must provide specific dates which makes the process of comparing fares, times and airlines time-consuming.

The price of round-the-world (RTW) tickets has remained fairly consistent over the past few years, though taxes and fuel surcharges have leapt up. You shouldn't count on getting much change from £1,000. Check www.roundtheworldflights.com (0845 347 0262) or Travel Nation in Hove, Sussex (0845 344 4225; www.travel-nation.co.uk) for ideas. RTW fares start at £699 for six stops departing London between April and June (plus taxes) and normally have a maximum validity of one year. The cheapest fares involve one or more gaps which you must cover overland. The most amazing RTW fare on offer at the time of writing was with Air New Zealand (available through Travelmood): London – Los Angeles – Auckland – Hong Kong – London for £639 including tax. Twenty-eight-year-old Tara Leaver splashed out on an ambitious RTW route with the One World Alliance (British Airways, Air New Zealand, etc.) for about £1,300 including Central America, South America, Easter Island, Tahiti, New Zealand, Australia and South East Asia. Apart from her first month of volunteering in Costa Rica (April 2006) which she had pre-arranged, she didn't want to over-plan the rest of her year off. The typical RTW deal imposes a mileage limit of 28,000 miles so you will have to make some careful calculations. Another tip for finding the cheapest available fares is to tap into the expat community of the country to which you would like to fly. For example the cheapest flights from Toronto to Korea are probably found among the many travel agencies to be found in the city's 'Little Korea' district on Bloor Street West.

The cheapest longhaul flights are probably available from airlines like Aeroflot or Biman Bangla-desh, which are considered dubious by cautious and conservative types. East European carriers (like Tarom) and Asian carriers (like Eva Airways) are often worth investigating for low fares, although British Airways, Air New Zealand and other mainstream carriers have good promotional fares some-times to rival the lesser-known airlines' fares. Flying on obscure airlines is guaranteed to be more interesting than flying on Air Canada or British Airways. When Sarah Spiller fell in love with Sri Lanka after joining a turtle conservation project and persuaded her husband that they should buy a holiday house there, she made several trips on Sri Lankan Airlines and felt that she was already on holiday the minute she stepped aboard. The travel agency Eastways (020-7247 2424; www.eastwaystravel. com) has the franchise for discounting tickets for Aeroflot, the Russian airline which has flights from London to Beijing or Seoul starting at £350-£390 return plus tax of about £140.

Some of the principal agencies specialising in longhaul travel are listed here. All of these offer a wide choice of fares including RTW. Telephone bookings are possible, though these agencies are often so busy that it can be difficult to get through. Although STA specialise in deals for students and under-26s, they can assist anybody.

STA Travel has about 65 branches in the UK and more than 450 worldwide. Offer low cost flights, accommodation, insurance, car hire, round-the-world tickets, overland travel, adventure tours, ski, and gap year travel. For bookings and enquiries call STA Travel on 0871 230 0040 or log on at www.statravel.co.uk to find fares and check availability. You can request a quote by email or make an appointment at your nearest branch.

Trailfinders Ltd, 194 Kensington High St, London W8 7RG (0845 058 5858 worldwide; 0845 050

5940 Europe); www.trailfinders.com. Also more than a dozen branches in UK cities plus Dublin and five in Australia.

Flight Centre has branches around the UK (0870 499 0040; www.flightcentre.co.uk).

Journey Latin America, 12-13 Heathfield Terrace, Chiswick, London W4 4JE (020-8747 3108; www.journeylatinamerica.co.uk). A fully-bonded agency which specialises in travel to and around all of Latin America. Consistently offers the lowest fares and the most expertise. One of the best flight deals at the time of writing was on Iberia to Rio or Caracas for about £550.

Marco Polo Travel, 24A Park St, Bristol BS1 5JA (0117-929 4123; www.marcopolotravel.co.uk). Discounted airfares worldwide.

North South Travel, Moulsham Mill Centre, Parkway, Chelmsford, Essex CM2 7PX (01245 608291; www.northsouthtravel.co.uk). Discount travel agency that donates all its profits to projects in the developing world.

Quest Travel has offices in Kingston, York and Brighton (0870 444 5552; www.questtravel.com).

South American Experience Ltd, 47 Causton St, Pimlico, London SW1P 4AT (020-7976 5511; www.southamericanexperience.co.uk). Latin American specialist with good customer service.

Travelbag, 3-5 High St, Alton, Hants. GU34 1TL (0870 814 4440; www.travelbag.co.uk). Originally Australia and New Zealand specialist, now owned by ebookers.

Travelmood, London office: 214 Edgware Road, London W2 1DH (08700 664566; www.travel-mood.com). Branches in Islington, Guildford, Leeds, Liverpool and Dundee.

Once you accept a price, check that the fare will not be increased between paying the deposit (typically £50 or £75) and handing over the balance in exchange for the ticket; if the agency is unable to make such a guarantee, ask for a written promise that you can reclaim the deposit in the event of a fare increase. Buying dodgy tickets is always worrying since it is impossible to grasp all the complexities of international air travel. Hand over the balance only when you are satisfied that the dates and times agree with what you anticipated. Roger Blake was pleased with the round-the-world ticket he bought from STA for £940 that took in Johannesburg, Australia and South America. But once he embarked he wanted to stay in Africa longer than he had anticipated and wanted to alter the onward flight dates:

> *That is the biggest problem of having an air ticket. I had planned for six months in Africa but I've already spent five months in only three countries. I have been into the British Airways office here in Kampala to try my verbal skills but have been told the 12-month period of validity is non-negotiable. How stupid I was to presume I would get a refund when it states clearly on the back of the ticket that they may be able to offer refunds/credit. A lesson for me and a warning to future 'work your wayers' to check before they buy whether or not the ticket is refundable/extendable.*

In the US, check the discount flight listings in the back of the travel sections of the *New York Times* and *Los Angeles Times*. Discounted tickets are available online from Air Treks in San Francisco (1-877-247-8735; www.AirTreks.com) which specialises in multi-stop and round-the-world fares. By far the cheapest airfares from the US to Europe, Mexico, the Caribbean and Hawaii are available to people who are flexible about departure dates and destinations, and are prepared to travel on a standby basis. The passenger chooses a block of possible dates (up to a four-day 'window') and preferred destinations. The company then tries to match these requirements with empty airline seats being released at knock-down prices. Air-Tech (212-219-7000; www.airtech.com) offers transatlantic fares starting at $239 one way from the east coast and $299 from the west coast, excluding tax; plus an optional FedEx delivery charge of $18 and possible fuel surcharges departing Europe of up to €150.

From the UK to Europe it is generally cheaper to fly on an off-peak no-frills flight out of Stansted, Luton or a regional airport than it is by rail or bus. Almost all bookings are made online and telephone bookings attract a higher fare. Airlines like *Easyjet* (0905 821 0905; www.easyjet.com), *Ryanair* (0871 246 0000; www.ryanair.com), *Bmibaby* (0871 224 0224; www.bmibaby.com), Jet2 based at Leeds Airport (0871 226 1737; www.jet2.com), and Thomsonfly (0870 1900 737; www.thomsonfly.com) connect the UK with a large range of European cities and beyond. No-frills flying has been available in North America for some time, especially through Southwest Airlines based in Dallas (www.southwest.com). Normally the cheapest advance purchase coast-to-coast fares in the US are about $200, though Southwest were advertising a fare of $150 including taxes between Philadelphia and Los Angeles (autumn 2006). Meanwhile this style of flying has spread to the continent and discount airlines have proliferated like Air Berlin and Germanwings in Germany and Wizz Air in Poland at www.wizzair.com. To check which discount airlines operate to which European destinations, log on to www.flycheapo.com. The idea has spread to Australia with Richard Branson's Virgin Blue (www.virginblue.com.au) and to Canada with airlines like CanJet and WestJet offering cheap domestic flights. In October 2006 a new no-frills carrier launched longhaul flights between the UK and Hong Kong; check Oasis Hong Kong Airlines fares at www.oasishongkong.com. This is the airline that has been selling £109 flights to Hong Kong tax included but only to people over 55.

DRIVING

In some countries you might decide to buy a cheap car and hope that it lasts long enough for you to see the country. This worked well for Frank Schiller, a German traveller in Australia:

> *How about becoming a car owner yourself if you just wanna roll along for a while? After two successful months of hitching in Tasmania (including a combined Landrover and yacht lift to Maria Island), the three of us decided to change our means of transport. We bought a Holden off a Canadian guy for $500 which included insurance, a few spare parts, a tool kit and some snorkelling equipment. (I'd suggest buying a standard model rather than an E-type Jaguar for ease of finding spares.) After ten weeks and 10,000 kilometres, we sold it to a wrecker in Alice Springs for $250. So each of us had paid $80 for the car plus about $120 for petrol – all in all a much better bargain than a bus pass.*

A camper van is also an appealing idea, especially if you are interested in chasing fruit harvests around. It is possible to pick up a reliable vehicle for less than £1,000 if you're lucky.

AUSTRALIANS LIKE BEN HOCKLEY ARE DEVOTED VAN USERS:

My girlfriend and I were spending a lot of money looking for work in Spain so we decided we needed a campervan to help cut the accommodation costs. Vans are not very cheap in Spain and the casual relaxed attitude of the locals makes car hunting a nightmare. So we hopped a train to Amsterdam where I had learnt that vehicles were 40% cheaper. It was true and after three weeks we had an old Bedford camper for about £1,000. Life in the van was great, we could just park on any street and we had a home for the night.

An informal van market takes place daily in London on York Way at Market Road, N7 near the Caledonian Road tube station. You might also check ads in *Auto Trader, Exchange & Mart* and *LOOT* or if starting in London on www.gumtree.com, London's online community.

Those who own their own vehicle might consider taking it with them. Certainly a car or motorcycle on the continent will make life easier when it comes to visiting potential employers, especially in the countryside. On the negative side, it will be an expensive luxury (even if petrol is cheaper on the continent than in the UK) and a serious encumbrance if you decide to travel outside continental Europe. If you are considering taking your car, contact your local AA or RAC office for information about International Driving Permits, motor insurance, green cards, etc. To compare fares on car ferries, log on to www.aferry.to or www.allferries.co.uk.

HITCH-HIKING

Over the past generation, hitch-hiking has fallen by the wayside (so to speak), and is practised now by only a few diehards, even though it is not only the best travel bargain around, but the most rewarding as well. The disappearance of hitching may be because young travellers and students are generally more affluent and also because of a heightened sense of paranoia (though the dangers remain infinitesimal). However there are still enough people out there interested to support a number of websites including www.hitchhikers.org which has an up-to-date ride board. Many shared lifts these days are fixed up via online marketplaces ahead of time, sometimes referred to as digital hitch-hiking. Another interesting website is www.digihitch.com.

In the experience of many travellers, hitching is cheap, safe and fascinating (and what else could anyone ask for?). The uncertainty of the destination is one of its great attractions to the footloose traveller. While hitching from France to Germany in pursuit of work, Kevin Boyd got a lift with a Russian truck bound for Leningrad. He was tempted to stay for the whole trip but, as the lorry averaged 35km an hour on the autoroute, he decided to stick with his original idea. Hitch-hiking has one positive virtue for job seekers: you can sound out the driver for advice on local job opportunities. Friendly drivers often go miles out of their way and may even ask in villages about work possibilities on your behalf, as happened to Andrew Winwood in Switzerland during the *vendange*. Lorry drivers often know of temporary jobs.

Hitch-hiking is also good for the environment. As long ago as 1998, a UK government report was published to promote car-sharing. One of the suggested measures was to introduce hitch-hiker pick-up zones at motorway junctions which would be brightly lit and possibly equipped with closed circuit TVs. Special hitching spots in the Netherlands are called *liftershalte*. Hitch-hiking, like any form of transport, has its dangers, but that is not a sufficient argument for a wholesale ban. The existence of road rage and air rage, of attacks on or derailment of trains, does not result in mass avoidance of these modes of travel. By following a few rules the risks of hitch-hiking can be minimised. Never accept a lift from a driver who seems drunk, drowsy or suspicious. Women should try not to hitch alone. A small dose of paranoia is not a bad thing.

But try to put the risks into perspective. It is worth mentioning that my friend Simon Calder, author of the now out-of-print *Hitch-hikers Manual: Britain* and *Europe: A Manual for Hitch-hikers,* has found cycling in London a far more dangerous and damaging pursuit than thumbing lifts (and has lived to become the Travel Editor of the *Independent* newspaper). Usually the worst danger is of boredom and discouragement when you have a long wait. It is of course a game of patience. Eventually you will get a lift, but whether you have the stamina to wait for it is another matter.

In some Western countries organisations fix drivers up with cost-sharing passengers upon payment of a small fee (see the section on Europe below). An interesting variation is to prearrange a ride by talking to lorry drivers at local depots, lorry parks, truckers' cafés, pubs or wherever you see them. However in these nervous times when a stranger is considered a terrorist until proven innocent, this will take more patience and luck than it used to do.

TRAIN

The conventional wisdom is that trains are preferable to buses because they allow you to walk around or lie down on long journeys. Anyone who has experienced travelling unreserved on Indian trains or on long distance Italian trains in high summer (where theft is rife) will be aware of the limitations of this generalisation. Besides which, the traveller working his or her way around the world is more interested in financial considerations than in ones of comfort. But in areas which have a dreadfully creaky and overcrowded rail service (running to a calendar rather than a timetable), it may well be the cheapest way of getting around. Even in developed nations, you may find rail fares rivalling the coach, especially if you are eligible for discounts. Rail passes are generally not much use to job-seeking travellers since they benefit people who want to do a great deal of travelling.

For the Inter-Rail ticket, you must choose between continuous travel for 22 days or one month, and bear in mind that seat reservations will cost extra. Current prices for the under-26s are £226 for 22 days and £292 for a month anywhere in Europe. These are the prices if bought in the UK, for example from Rail Europe (08705 848848; www.raileurope.co.uk); prices in euros bought on the continent are lower.

Other youth and student discounts can be very useful; for example the *Wochenendticket* (weekend ticket) in Germany is valid for the whole country on Saturdays and Sundays but only on regional trains. It costs €35 for up to five people which means that you can get from the Austrian to the Danish border for less than £5 each.

The Thomas Cook *Overseas Timetable* is the bible for overland travellers outside Europe; within Europe, consult the *European Timetable*, updated monthly, both for £13.99 but discounted on www.thomascooktimetables.com. One of the wonders of the internet is the site maintained by the 'Man in Seat 61' (www.seat61.com) which carries masses of information about overland train travel and tickets.

Specialist agents can sell tickets; for example German Railways (Deutsche Bahn) sells tickets to Germany and other European countries from its office in London (0870 243 5363; www.bahn.co.uk). For specialist services for Australia, North America and Japan try International Rail (0870 751 5000; www.international-rail.com) and for European routes Trainseurope (0900 195 0101; www.trainseurope.com). Great Rail Journeys (01904 521900; www.greatrail.com) and Rail Choice (0870 165 7300; www.railchoice.co.uk) can book most rail journeys.

COACH

In many areas of the world such as Nepal and Papua New Guinea, public road transport is the only way to get around the country short of flying. Fortunately this monopoly of the travel market is not generally reflected in high fares, usually because of competing companies. Such free enterprise is wonderfully apparent at the Topkapi Gate Bus Station in Istanbul where salesmen for a host of competing companies call out their destinations and prices. Bus prices are below a penny per mile in much of the Third World (possibly to compensate for the purgatory of non-stop Kung Fu videos in some parts of the world). Except where smooth air-conditioned buses provide an alternative to sub-third class rail travel, coaches are generally less expensive than trains. The Thomas Cook *Overseas Timetable* is valuable for coach as well as train travellers.

One of the most interesting revolutions in youth travel has been the explosion of backpackers' bus services which are hop-on hop-off coach services following prescribed routes. These can be found in New Zealand, Australia, South Africa (BazBus), Ireland, Scotland, England and the continent. Generally they are not really cheap enough to serve as a jobseeker's preferred mode of transport. For example a Flexitrip pass on Busabout Europe (020-7950 1661; www.busabout.com) costs £239 and allows six stops within the whole operating season May to October; many other permutations are available. For travel on the Eurolines network, see the section on Europe below.

BICYCLE

CYCLING IS NOT ONLY HEALTHY AND FREE, IT CAN SIMPLIFY THE BUSINESS OF FINDING WORK, AS ADAM COOK DISCOVERED IN FRANCE:
Looking for work by bicycle is one of the very best methods as it allows you free unlimited travel far from the big towns and the competition. You can so easily visit the small villages and farms, some of which are off the beaten track.

In addition, employers may realise that people who have been cycling for a while are at least moderately fit and may choose them for the job, ahead of the flabbier vehicle-bound competition. In many parts of the world you will also become an object of fascination, which can only aid your job-finding chances. If you do decide to travel extensively by bicycle, you might consider joining the Cyclists' Touring Club based in Guildford (0870 873 0060; www.ctc.org.uk) which provides free technical, legal and touring information to members as well as third party insurance; membership costs £12 if you are a student under 26, £34 otherwise.

EUROPE

The European landmass is one of the most expensive areas of the world to traverse. Not all European countries are equally hitchable: Greece and Italy are fine – if you're blonde and female; Portugal is good, Spain is dreadful, Germany is far easier than France, while Ireland, Denmark and Switzerland are excellent, and so on. One of the best is Poland, as confirmed by Jakob Steixner, where many years ago the government encouraged lift-sharing by rewarding drivers, and the tradition continues.

Often lifts can be arranged informally without having to stand out in the weather. Ride-sharing can be fixed up via websites as mentioned above or by community agencies, often called 'Allostop' where you will have to make a contribution to the driver's expenses, e.g. €50 for Amsterdam to Warsaw. Check notice boards in hostels or youth travel bureaux or try websites such as http://europe.bugride.com, which publicises long-distance rides offered and sought on its site. There are dozens of lift-sharing outlets across Europe, especially in Germany, where there are Citynetz offices in Berlin, Düsseldorf, Freiburg, Hamburg, Munich, etc. Most require you to register, which is free in some cases or costs €10-20 in others.

Here are some details of European agencies:

France: Allostop, 30 rue Pierre Sémard, 75009 Paris (1-53 20 42 42; allostop@wanadoo.fr; www. allostop.net). Prices are set according to number of journeys e.g. €35 for up to ten trips in two years, or €7 for one journey (or €3 if it is less than 150km).

Belgium: Taxistop/Eurostop, 28 rue Fossé-aux-Loups, 1000 Brussels (+32 70-22 22 92; www. taxistop.be). Also has offices in Ghent, Brussels and Ottignies. Subscribing is free and payments to drivers are negotiated on an ad hoc basis (probably about €2.50 per 100km.

Germany: Citynetz-Mitzfahrzentrale – www.citynetz-mitfahrzentrale.de. Website gives contact details of offices in Berlin, Hannover and seven other cities. Prices are calculated at 3-4 Eurocents per kilometre.

Matches can seldom be made straightaway, so this system is of interest to those who can plan ahead.

On the whole the railways of Europe are expensive and as noted above Inter-Railing is not ideally suited to travellers who want to stop long enough to pick up work. It is almost always cheaper to book a no-frills flight from Stansted or Luton. The explosion of competition on European routes has seen some amazingly low fares, though taxes and add-ons make it almost impossible to spend less than £35-£40 on a return flight. As well as checking Ryanair and easyjet, don't forget foreign no-frills carriers like Air Berlin (www.airberlin.com) and Norwegian Air Shuttle (www.norwegian.no).

Eurolines is the group name for 32 independent coach operators serving 500 destinations in all European countries from Ireland to Romania. Promotional prices start at £30 return for London-Amsterdam if booked 7 days in advance. Bookings can be made online at www.nationalexpress.com/eurolines or by phoning 08705 808080. So called 'funfares' mean that some off-season fares from the UK are even lower, e.g. £6 to Brussels or Paris.

For smaller independent coach operators, check advertisements in London magazines like *TNT*. For example Capital Express (London W11; 020-7243 0488; www.capitalexpress.cz) runs daily between London and Prague, Brno, Olomouc or Ostrava; fares start at £43 single, £63 return. Poltours links the UK and Poland for £50 one way, £75 return.

NORTH AMERICA

Incredibly, the price of flying across the Atlantic has been steadily decreasing over the past decade, though with increased taxes, it is difficult to find much less than £250. Competition is fiercest and therefore prices lowest on the main routes between London and New York and Los Angeles/San Francisco. In many cases, summer fares will be twice as high as winter ones. One-way fares are also available to eastern seaboard cities like Washington and Boston. Outside summer and the Christmas period you should have no problems getting a seat; at peak times, a reliable alternative is to buy a discounted ticket on one of the less fashionable carriers which fly to New York, such as Air India or El Al. The USA and Canada share the longest common frontier in the world, which gives some idea of the potential problems and expense of getting around. You will want to consider Driveaway (see the *United States* chapter) and also bus and air travel which are both cheaper than in Europe. In the US, consult any branch of STA (1-877-777-8717) and in Canada look for an office of Travel Cuts, the youth and student travel specialist (www.travelcuts.com). If you intend to travel widely in the States check out air passes. Hitch-hiking in the USA is often unnerving and sometimes fraught with danger, danger not only from crazy drivers but also from the law, especially where 'No Hitch-hiking' signs abound. It is a more reasonable proposition in Canada. Ride-sharing makes more sense on this continent. Try www.erideshare.com as mentioned above. The system of Allo-Stop is well developed in the province of Québec but has been ruled illegal in Ontario after complaints were received from coach operators; check www.allostop.com for up-to-date information.

South of the Canadian border, bus passes (Ameripass) are a travel bargain for people who want to cover a lot of ground. Greyhound has no office in the UK but their US-Canada pass can be bought through STA and a few others such as Western Air Travel in Devon (0870 330 1100; www.westernair. co.uk). In 2007, Greyhound (www.greyhound.com) was offering 7, 15, 30 and 60 day Discovery passes valid on the whole North American network for £167, £245, £308 and £380. Once you are in the US timetable and fare information is available 24 hours a day on the toll-free number 1-800-231-2222.

Megabus in the US operates as it does in the UK; tickets can be booked only online and if you do it in advance you get the best fares. At the moment their hub is Chicago serving Minneapolis, St Louis, Cleveland and a few other cities in the Midwest; a sample one-way fare for the four and a half hour journey from Detroit to Chicago starts at a mere $15.

Other forms of transport in the USA are probably more expensive but may have their own attractions, such as the trips run by Green Tortoise (494 Broadway, San Francisco, California 94133; 800-867-8647; www.greentortoise.com) which use vehicles converted to sleep about 35 people and which make interesting detours and stopovers. There may even be an option to swap your labour for a free ride.

The deregulation of US domestic airlines some years ago resulted in lunatic discounting. Southwest Airlines based in Dallas (www.southwest.com) is one of the better known discount companies offering cheap fares and no-frills service. Normally the cheapest advance purchase coast-to-coast fares are about $200. The best advice within the USA is to ask locals and study local newspapers, as fare wars are usually fought using full page advertisements. Airtech mentioned above now specialises in flights to Hawaii booked up to 14 days in advance, from $129 each way from California to Maui, Honolulu and Lihue. Attempts to revive long-distance train travel in the US have not been terribly successful and several grand old routes are threatened with closure. Amtrak (1-800-USA-RAIL/872-7245; www.amtrak.com) offers some good value rail passes such as 15 days around the western half of the country for $215 low season or 30 days for $280. The basic three-and-a-half day train trip from Toronto to Vancouver costs about C$600 in the summer, $454 off-season; student discounts are available. The Via Rail infoline in Canada is 1-888-842-7245 (www.viarail.ca).

For accommodation in North America, see the hostel list at www.backpackers.ca.

LATIN AMERICA

In the low seasons of January to May and October to November, you can get from London to South America for £200-£300 one way, though this is rarely the best way to do it because international tickets bought out there are very expensive. Having a return ticket makes it much easier to cross borders. Open-dated returns are available as are open jaw tickets (where you fly into one point and back from another). It might be possible to extend these even if you decide to stay longer than a year; Nick Branch had an Alitalia ticket which he extended more than once for a $100 fee.

A fully-bonded agency that specialises in travel to and around this area of the world is Journey Latin America (London and Manchester; 020-8747 3108; www.journeylatinamerica.co.uk) who consistently offer the lowest fares and the most expertise. Another advantage is that they deal exclusively with Latin America and hence are the best source of up-to-date travel information. One of the best deals at the time of writing was a six-month return to Rio on Air Portugal for £517. A plethora of airpasses is also available which can be cheaper if bought at the same time as your transatlantic ticket. Another specialist in the field is South American Experience in Victoria (London) who offer an excellent service as well and whose prices should be compared (0870 499 0683; www.southamericanexperience.co.uk). Overland tours with companies like Tucan Travel (www.tucantravel.com) can provide a fun and enlightened intro-duction to the continent.

Taxes are levied on international flights within South America: the cheapest way to fly from one capital to another (assuming you have plenty of time) is to take a domestic flight (within, say, Brazil), cross the border by land and then buy another domestic ticket (within, say, Peru). The alternatives include the remnants of a British-built railway system and the ubiquitous bus, both of which are extremely cheap and interesting. A rough estimate of the price of bus travel in South America is $2+ for every hour of travel.

Among the most reliable travel guides to the continent is the warhorse *South American Handbook* published annually by Footprint Handbooks (2007, £20). For information on travel in Latin America join South American Explorers. They maintain clubhouses in Lima, Cusco, Quito and Buenos Aires. The US office is at 126 Indian Creek Rd, Ithaca, NY 14850 (607-277-0488; www.saexplorers.org) and member-ship costs $50, or $80 per couple. In addition to travel information they have also developed extensive databases of voluntary and teaching jobs for members to access.

AFRICA

Flights to Cairo are advertised from £150 single, £200 return, while the special offers to Nairobi start as low as £280 single, £395 return. A specialist agency is the Africa Travel Centre (21 Leigh St, London WC1H 9QX; 0845 450 1520; www.africatravel.co.uk). Melhart Travel in Manchester (0870 787 4467; www.melharttravel.com) specialises in South Africa. A return to Johannesburg in the low season (April-July 1st) was costing from £415 and Cape Town £450 at the time of writing.

The overland routes are fraught with difficulties, and careful research must be done before setting off via the Sahara (the route through the Sudan is of course impossible at present). Jennifer McKibben, who spent some time in East Africa, recommends trying to negotiate a cheap seat in one of the overland expedition vehicles which are so much in evidence in that part of the world, assuming *'half their number have stormed off the bus or truck, unable to bear each other any longer'*.

ASIA

The famous hippy overland route to Nepal has been problematical for a very long time now, though not impossible. Although Afghanistan is still off-limits, it is possible to cross Iran into Pakistan (a very rigorous but very cheap trip, assuming you can get a transit visa for Iran). Most travellers simply take advantage of the competitive discount flight market from London to Asian destinations. For example the cheapest quoted return price London to Mumbai is £335 including tax on Etihad Airways (the airline of the UAE). The cheapest advertised flights to Bangkok (early 2007) were £180 one-way, £320 return. The price of flights to Japan has dropped significantly in the past few years, especially if you are willing to fly on Aeroflot. In London a wide range of travel agents advertises cheap fares to Asia.

Once you're installed in Asia, travel is highly affordable. The railways of the Indian sub-continent are a fascinating social phenomenon and also dirt cheap. Throughout Asia, airfares are not expensive, particularly around the discount triangle of Bangkok, Hong Kong and Singapore. The notable exception to the generalisation about cheap public transport in Asia is Japan.

Travel within the People's Republic of China can initially be exasperating as you struggle with the inscrutable bureaucracy and the utterly incomprehensible nature of stations and airports (where little allowance is made for those who do not understand Chinese characters). But like most things in the East, once you come to terms with the people and their way of life, travelling once more becomes a pleasurable experience.

With upheavals in Russia, the Trans-Siberian rail journey is not as cheap as it used to be. Anyone who has read any of the abundant literature of rail travel like Paul Theroux's *Great Railway Bazaar* and Eric Newby's *The Big Red Train Ride* about the Trans-Siberian may have had their appetite whetted and want to take the train between Moscow and Beijing. Specialist travel agents can arrange the Trans-Siberian trip for you, for instance the excellent travel company *Regent Holidays* (0870 499 0911; www.regent-holidays.co.uk) which pioneered tourism in Cuba, Eastern Europe and Central Asia. For lesser known routes such as the Silk Route Railway through Kazakhstan and China, you will have to put it together yourself, possibly with the help of www.seat61.com mentioned above. If you are already in China, you can simply organise the ticket and visas yourself as Barry O'Leary did:

> *I had discovered that if you book the Trans-Siberian on your own and don't pay for an agency to rip you off and organise everything yourself it's actually really cheap. Sure you have some hassle getting visas for China, Mongolia and Russia but isn't that all part of the fun? The total cost to get from Beijing to Moscow with three visas was only about £250, not bad for six days on a train and some tasty meat and celery stuff.*

Alternatively you can use a Chinese agency such as Monkey Business located in Beijing's Red House Hotel (www.monkeyshrine.com). For detailed advice, see the *Trans-Siberian Handbook* published by Trailblazer at £12.99.

AUSTRALASIA

Buying a tourist visa for Australia is compulsory. The paperless visa, the ETA (Electronic Travel Authority), must be obtained via a private agency like Visas Australia or the Australian Immigration Department's website (www.eta.immi.gov.au) which will incur a fee of A$20. The dispensing of visitor visas has in essence been privatised and specialist visa providers can charge a fee of their choice (none of which is passed on to the Australian government). Among the cheaper providers are www.fastozvisa.com (0800 096 4749) which charges $12/£7.50 and www.australiavisas.com which charges $18.

Tourism Australia delivers quite a bit of hard information and useful links (www.australia.com). The backpackers' guide *Australia & New Zealand Independent Travellers' Guide* from *TNT* magazine (London and Sydney) is free because it is funded by advertising; you can read it online at www.tntmagazine.com (click on 'TNT Guides'). Per mile, the flight to the Antipodes is cheaper than most. Malaysia Airlines often turns out to be the cheapest, although Qantas has been competing strongly of late with promotional fares of less than £600 return available through specialists like Austravel (0870 166 2020; www.austravel.com).

Your transport problems are by no means over when you land in Perth or Sydney. The distances in Australia may be much greater than you are accustomed to and so you will have to give some thought to how you intend to get around. Richard Branson's Virgin Blue (www.virginblue.com.au) has some good deals and his Pacific Blue flies across the Tasman to New Zealand. Sample Blue fares in 2007 were A$120 Sydney to Cairns and A$150 Melbourne to Christchurch (via Brisbane) plus A$100 tax. Compare also the no-frills domestic airline Jetstar (www.jetstar.com.au), a subsidiary of Qantas. Substantial discounts are offered on Qantas domestic flights to overseas visitors who buy domestic flights in conjunction with their international flight. Price wars are frequent. At the time of writing Qantas was undercutting Air New Zealand on domestic flights in New Zealand by charging NZ$64 one-way Auckland-Wellington. Also check out Freedom Air (www.freedomair.co.nz) which flies into the smaller North Island cities of Palmerston North and Hamilton.

If you plan a major tour of Australia you might consider purchasing a Greyhound coach pass along a pre-set route (13 14 99 or +61-7-4690 9950; www.greyhound.com.au). Sample prices are A$432 for the nearly 3,000km trip between Sydney and Cairns and the 10,000km all-Australia pass costing A$1,275 valid for 12 months which includes the 10% discount offered to backpackers with a YHA or other hostel or student card. If you just want to get from one coast to another as quickly as possible and qualify for the very cheapest deals, you will pay from A$500 one way on the coach or train (excluding berth and meals). Students and backpackers are eligible for a very good deal on the railways: unlimited travel on the great transcontinental routes for six months costs A$590 (www.railaustralia.com.au/rail_passes.htm).

A multiplicity of private operators has sprung up to serve the backpacking market such as Oz Experience (which has a reputation as a party bus) and Wayward Bus. The hop-on hop-off service in New Zealand is the Magic Travellers Network (+64 9-358 5600; www.magicbus.co.nz) which picks up from hostels around New Zealand. Writing from New South Wales, Geertje Korf passed on the following warning: *'A guy I met from Canada arrived here on a bus whose driver had promised him guaranteed work for up to A$100 a day. He paid A$70 for transport from Sydney and had the impression that he would be taken to an orchard, shown where to pitch his tent, etc. But instead the driver simply dropped him off at the job centre. He could have saved money by just catching the ordinary bus and walking.'*

Having your own transport is a great advantage when job-hunting in Australia. Some places have second-hand cars and camper vans for sale which they will buy back at the end of your stay, for example Boomerang Cars in Adelaide (261 Currie St, 0414-882559; www.boomerangcars.com.au) or Travellers Auto Barn in Sydney, Melbourne, Brisbane, Cairns, Perth and Darwin (www.travellers-autobarn.com). Expect to pay A$2,000+ for an old car (like a gas-guzzling Ford Falcon) and more for a camper van; the more you spend the better your chance of its lasting the distance and being saleable at the end of your stay. Car hire is expensive, but occasionally 'relocations' are available, i.e. hire cars that need to be returned to their depots. Just pick up the *Yellow Pages* and phone through the rental companies and ask for relocation deals which is exactly what Roger Blake did when he wanted to travel from Adelaide to Melbourne:

The Great Ocean Road is renowned as one of the most scenic drives in the world and I was determined not to see it from a tour bus window. I phoned a hundred and one rental companies looking for a relocation (taking a vehicle back to its state depot due to one-way rental demands). I got lucky because they desperately needed one to leave the next day. Only a $1 per day rental and so desperate that they even gave me a $100 *for fuel. So I spent the following three days on my own in a flash 4/5 berth Mercedes-Benz motorhome on the spectacular Great Ocean Road along the coast of Victoria. The whole drive is dangerously scenic. And the cost to me? A whopping A$63!*

Apollo Motorhomes lists the $1 campervan relocations it has available on its website www.apollocamper. com.au (info@apollocamper.com). The best places to start are Cairns, Darwin, Adelaide and Broome where drivers are given $250-$350 worth of fuel in addition. Many vehicles need repositioning from Christchurch back to Auckland and often the ferry fee is thrown in. If you can't afford the luxury of organised transport or buying your own vehicle, you might be drawn to the idea of hitch-hiking. A coast to coast journey won't take you much less than a week, so it's a major undertaking. Be careful about being dropped on isolated stretches of the road across the Nullarbor Plain where, without water, you might just expire before the next vehicle comes along. On the other hand, you might be lucky and get one of those not uncommon lifts which covers 3200km in 96 hours.

Many women travellers have expressed their reluctance to travel alone with a long-distance lorry driver in remote areas, especially after the well-publicised backpacker murders a few years ago. The Queensland coastal road is notoriously dangerous. Violence is rare, but if you are unlucky you might be evicted from the truck unless you comply with the driver's wishes. All backpackers' hostels are a good bet for finding drivers going your way, provided you are able to wait for a suitable ride. Try also the lift-sharing forum on www.backpackingaround.com.au.

You need not confine yourself to cars and lorries for hitching. Adrian McCay hitched a lift on a private plane from remote Kununurra to Mildura. While working at a remote property in Western Australia, David Irvine hitched a couple of lifts with the flying doctor service. Earlier in his travels he got stranded in Norseman after a truck ride across the Nullarbor. Here he met an aboriginal swagman who advised him to hop a freight which he did, which turned out to be a coal train. Suddenly there was a very rare rainstorm which turned the coal dust on which he was sitting in his open hopper to disgusting sludge.

Once in New Zealand it is difficult to imagine a country more favourable to hitch-hikers and budget travellers with a network of cheap and cheerful hostels and mountain huts for 'trampers'. Camping on beaches, fields and in woodlands is generally permitted. Tranzscenic railways has some good low season deals on the South Island, e.g. NZ$59 from Christchurch to Picton (0800 872467; www.tranzscenic. co.nz) and also offers 20% student discounts.

TRAVELLERS' HEALTH

No matter what country you are heading for, you should obtain the Department of Health leaflet T7.1 *Health Advice for Travellers* (updated May 2006). This leaflet should be available from any post office or doctor's surgery. Alternatively you can request a free copy on the Health Literature Line 0870 155 5455 or read it online at www.dh.gov.uk, which also has country-by-country details.

The old E111 certificate of entitlement to medical treatment within Europe has been superseded by the European Health Insurance Card (EHIC). In the first phase of introduction, the new card will cover health care for short stays. By 2008, the electronic card will take the place of the current E128 and E119 which cover longer stays. This reciprocal cover is extended only to emergency treatment.

If you have a pre-existing medical condition it's important to anticipate what you might require in a crisis. Ask your GP or specialist support group for advice before you leave. Under extreme climatic conditions chronic or pre-existing conditions can be aggravated. Try to ascertain how easy it will be to access medicines on your trip, whether you'll be able to carry emergency supplies with you and how far you will be from specialist help. Always carry medications in their original containers and as a precaution you might carry a note from your doctor with an explanation of the drugs you're carrying and the relevant facts of your medical history. This could also include details of any allergies for example an intolerance of penicillin. This might be of use if you are involved in an accident or medical emergency.

In an age of mass communication it is usually possible to manage a medical condition while travelling or erect a safety net. If you plan to travel to an area with poor medical standards and unreliable blood screening, you might want to consider equipping yourself or your group with sterile syringes and needles. The Department of Travel Medicine at the Hospital for Tropical Diseases recommends that you carry a specially prepared sterile needle kit in case local emergency treatment requires injections; MASTA (see below) sells these for £17-£31.

Any visits beyond the developed world, particularly to tropical climates, require careful preparation. You will face the risk of contracting malaria or water-borne diseases like typhoid and cholera. You will need to provide your medical practitioner with precise details about where you intend to travel. Visit a travel medical centre at least a month before departure because some immunisations like those for yellow fever must be given well in advance. Expert medical advice is widely available on how to avoid tropical illness, so you should take advantage of modern medicine to protect yourself. And be prepared to pay for the necessary inoculations which are not normally covered by the NHS. It is always worth asking at your own surgery since if they are able to give good advice (and the internet has made that possible for any doctor worth his or her salt), the injections may be considerably cheaper than at a private specialist clinic where you are likely to pay between £30 and £50 per vaccine.

SPECIALIST ADVICE

Increasingly, people are carrying out their own health research on the internet; check for example www.fitfortravel.scot.nhs.uk, www.tmb.ie and www.travelhealth.co.uk. The website of the World Health Organization, www.who.int/ith, has some information including a listing of the very few countries in which certain vaccinations are a requirement of entry.

A company that has become one of the most authoritative sources of travellers' health information in Britain is *MASTA* (enquiries@masta.org; www.masta.org). Calls to the Travellers' Health Line (0906 822 4100) are charged at 60p per minute (average cost of call £2). It maintains a database of the latest information on the prevention of tropical and other diseases, from which it dispenses practical advice on its website and helpline. It can provide personalised advice depending on your destinations, which can be either e-mailed or posted to you. Here you can find explanations about protection against malaria, guidelines on what to eat and drink, and how to avoid motion sickness, jet lag and sunburn. MASTA's network of travel clinics (which has taken over British Airways travel clinics) administers inoculations and, like their online shop, sells medical kits and other specialist equipment like water purifiers and survival tools. MASTA also co-operates with the Blood Care Foundation, a charity that aims to deliver properly screened blood and sterile transfusion equipment to members in an emergency.

Private specialist clinics abound in London but are thin on the ground elsewhere. A worldwide searchable listing of specialist travel clinics is maintained by the International Society of Travel Medicine (www.istm.org) though many countries are not included.

The Hospital for Tropical Diseases in central London (Mortimer Market Building, Capper Street, Tottenham Court Road, WC1E 6AU) offers appointments at its Travel Clinic (020-7388 9600) and operates an automated Travellers Healthline Advisory Service on 020-7950 7799 (www.thehtd.org) which charges 50p a minute (average phone call lasts about seven minutes).

Other travel clinics include Nomad Travel Clinics in several London locations including Victoria (020-7823 5823; www.nomadtravel.co.uk) and also in Bristol and Southampton. They offer walk-in appointments and ten-minute consultations that cost £5 (which can be deducted from the cost of vaccinations). The Royal Free Travel Health Centre at the Royal Free Hospital on Pond Street in London (020-7830 2885; www.travelclinicroyalfree.com) is a well-regarded private clinic, and the *Trailfinders Travel Clinic* (194 Kensington High Street; 020-7983 3999; www.trailfinders.com/clinic.htm) is long-established. The Fleet Street Travel Clinic (020-7353 5678; www.fleetstreetclinic.com) charges a whopping £45 for a 15-minute consultation. Several online shops compete for travellers' custom, among them Travelpharm (01395 233771; www.travelpharm.com), which carries an extensive range of mosquito nets, anti-malaria drugs, water purification equipment and travel accessories. The website carries lots of health information.

For routine travellers' complaints, it is worth looking at a general guide to travel medicine such as *Bugs, Bites and Bowels* by Dr Jane Wilson Howarth (Cadogan, 2006, £9.99) or *Traveller's Health: How to Stay Healthy Abroad* by Richard Dawood (OUP, £15.99). These books emphasise the necessity of avoiding tap water and recommend ways to purify your drinking water by filtering, boiling or chemical additives (iodine is more reliable than chlorine). MASTA and Nomad market various water purifiers; among the best are the 'Aquapure Traveller' (£40+) and the 'Trekker Travel Well' (£70). Tap water throughout Western Europe is safe to drink.

Americans seeking general travel health advice should ring the Center for Disease Control and Prevention Hotline in Atlanta on 1-877-394-8747; www.cdc.gov. CDC issues travel announcements for international travellers rated from mild to extreme, i.e. minimal risk to a recommendation that non-essential travel be completely avoided.

For advice on protecting your sexual health, Marie Stopes International (020-7574 7400; www.mariestopes.org.uk) is helpful. They publish a free guide to traveller's sexual health called the *Back Pocket Guide*. The government's free booklet *Drugs Abroad* and the National Drugs Helpline (0800 776600) can give information on drugs laws abroad.

MALARIA

Malaria is undoubtedly the greatest danger posed by visits to many tropical areas. The disease has been making a comeback in many parts of the world, due to the resistance of certain strains of mosquito to the pesticides and preventative medications which have been so extensively relied upon in the past. Because of increasing resistance, it is important to consult a specialist service as above. You can become better informed by looking at specialist websites such as www.hpa.org.uk/infections/topics_az/malaria/default.htm or www.preventingmalaria.info. You need to obtain the best information available to help you devise the most appropriate strategy for protection in the areas you intend to visit. Research indicates for example that the statistical chance of being bitten by a malarial mosquito in Thailand is once a year, but in Sierra Leone it rises to once a night. Start your research early since some courses of malaria prophylaxis need to be started up to three weeks before departure. It is always a good idea to find out in advance if you are going to suffer any side effects as well.

Falciparum malaria is potentially fatal. On average between 2,000 and 2,500 travellers return to the UK with malaria every year, and between ten and twenty will die. The two main drugs can be obtained over the counter: Chloroquine and Proguanil (brand name Paludrine). In regions resistant to these drugs, you will have to take both or a third line of defence such as Maloprim or Mefloquine (or Larium) available only on prescription. Because of possible side effects it is important that your doctor be able to vary the level of toxicity to match the risks prevalent in your destination. A relatively new (and expensive) drug called Malarone is used as an alternative to mefloquine or doxycycline, and is recommended for short trips to highly chloroquine-resistant areas. New drugs are being developed all the time and sometimes there is a time lag before they are licensed in the UK or USA. For example in her gap year in Madagascar, Karen Hedges twice contracted malaria but was quickly treated with an effective drug called Coartem, expensive by local standards, and not yet licensed in the UK.

Unfortunately these prophylactic medications are not foolproof, and even those who have scrupulously swallowed their pills before and after their trip as well as during it have been known to contract the disease. It is therefore essential to take mechanical precautions against mosquitoes. If possible, screen the windows and sleep under a permethrin-impregnated mosquito net since the offending mosquitoes feed between dusk and dawn. (Practise putting your mosquito net up before leaving home since some are tricky to assemble.) Some travellers have improvised with some netting intended for prams which takes up virtually no luggage space. If you don't have a net, cover your limbs at nightfall with light-coloured garments, apply insect repellent with the active ingredient DEET and sleep with a fan on to keep the air moving. Try to keep your room free of the insects too by using mosquito coils, vaporisers, etc.

Deet is strong enough to last many hours. Wrist and ankle bands impregnated with the chemical are available and easy to use. Cover your limbs as night falls (6pm on the equator). Wearing fine silk clothes discourages bites and keep the repellent topped up.

Prevention is vastly preferable to cure. It is a difficult disease to treat, particularly in its advanced stages. If you suffer a fever up to twelve months after returning home from a malarial zone, visit your doctor and mention your travels, even if you suspect it might just be flu.

FORMALITIES AT BORDERS

Whichever mode of transport you choose, there are a number of formalities that must be tackled before you set off, to ensure that your journey is not fraught with an unexpected range of disasters. Heightened security everywhere means that more time must be set aside for airports and borders.

VISAS

Outside the Schengen Area of Europe in which border controls have been largely abolished for EU nationals, you can't continue in one direction for very long before you are impeded by border guards demanding to see your papers. Post September 11th, immigration and security checks are tighter than ever before and many countries have imposed visa restrictions, particularly on North Americans in retaliation for all the new restrictions the US has implemented. Embassy websites are the best source of information or you can check online information posted by visa agencies. For example Thames Consular Services in London (www.thamesconsular.com) allows you to search visa requirements and costs for UK nationals visiting any country. An equivalent source of visa information in the US is Travisa (www.travisa. com) with offices in Washington, New York, Chicago, San Francisco, Miami and London. Travel Document

Express in the US (www.traveldocument.com) provides visa application forms that can be downloaded, and can process visa and passport applications; or try Travel Document Systems in Washington, New York and San Francisco (www.traveldocs.com).

Getting visas is a headache anywhere, and most travellers feel happier obtaining them in their home country. Set aside a chunk of your travel budget to cover the costs; to give just a few examples of charges for tourist visas for UK citizens applying in London: £30 for India, £30 for China, £11 for Jordan, £23 or £38 for Vietnam (depending on whether you have a letter of authorisation), £35 for Armenia, £45 for Pakistan, £50 for Rwanda, £43.50 for Nigeria. Requirements for American travellers are completely different, for example no visa is required for Haiti (nor for the majority of Latin American countries), $115 for Brazil, $65 for India, $55 for China (or $85 for rush issuance), $21.50 for Jordan, $70 for Vietnam, $105 for Nigeria, etc. Last-minute applications often incur a much higher fee, for example a Russian visa costs £30 if applied for three weeks in advance, but £80 for three-day processing. If you do not want to pin yourself down to entry dates, you may decide to apply for visas as you travel for example from a neighbouring country, which in many cases is cheaper, though may cause delays.

If you are short of time or live a long way from the Embassies in London, private visa agencies like Thames Consular mentioned above can undertake the footwork for you, at a price. Other visa agencies include the VisaService in London N1 (020-7833 2709; fax 020-7833 1857; www.visaservice.co.uk) and Global Visas (020-7009 3800; www.globalvisas.com). In addition to the fee charged by the country's embassy, there will be a service charge normally of £35-£45 per visa. Travel Document Systems in the US charges $45 per visa plus FedEx delivery charge. If you intend to cross a great many borders, especially on an overland trip through Africa, ensure that you have all the relevant documentation and that your passport contains as many blank pages as frontiers which you intend to cross. Travellers have been turned back purely because the border guard refused to use a page with another stamp on it. Details of work permit regulations and so on can be found in the country chapters in this book. See also the introductory section *Red Tape*.

Always reply simply and politely to any questions asked by immigration or customs officials. Roger Blake has a word of warning: *'Arriving in New Zealand was not really a problem other than a strange encounter with a customs officer: 'Are you bringing drugs into the country?' 'No!' 'Do you take drugs?' 'NO!' I reply. She asks 'Why not?' This is the kind of carefully planned (and corrupt) trap for would-be's that you occasionally come across. Anyway, no worries on my part.'*

MONEY

On arrival at a border, you may be asked to prove that a) you have enough to support yourself for the duration of your proposed stay, and b) that you have the means to leave the country without undermining the economy by engaging in unauthorised activities (e.g. working, changing money on the black market, smuggling, etc.). The authorities are more likely to take an interest in a scruffy impecunious looking backpacker. Sometimes border personnel wish to see proof of absurdly large sums such as $1,000 for each month of your proposed stay. Remember that well-dressed travellers who carry suitcases rather than rucksacks will be challenged less often. Because Michel Falardeau was travelling on one-way tickets without all that much money, he wore a business suit whenever he was due to meet an immigration official, and this worked for him on his round-the-world trip. You can get away with having less money if you have an onward ticket, and the names and addresses of residents whom you intend to visit.

There are several ways round the problem. Some travellers have gone so far as to declare the loss of their travellers cheques, in order to use the duplicate set as 'flash money'. As soon as the duplicates have done their duty at the border, the supposedly lost originals can then be burned. A less dramatic technique is to show off your range of credit cards and make sure you know how to log on to the balance online so that if necessary you can prove instantly that you are in credit.

Find out beforehand whether there is a departure tax. For example to fly out of Korea you must pay 3,000 won, Kenya you must pay the equivalent of US$20, Peru $30, Ecuador (Quito) $37.93, Hong Kong HK$120, Nepal 1,695 rupees ($25) and so on. This can be an unexpected nuisance or a total disaster. Information about transferring emergency funds from home is given in the chapter *In Extremis* at the end of this book.

WORKING A PASSAGE

Many people setting out on their world travels assume, not unreasonably, that a large chunk of their savings must inevitably be swallowed up by airlines, railways and shipping companies. This need not be so. With a little advance planning, a fair amount of bravado and a dose of good fortune you can follow the example of thousands of travellers who have successfully voyaged around the globe for next to nothing.

Hitch-hiking is one way of crossing landmasses (see *Travel*) though it has fallen so out of favour with the 21st-century traveller that alternatives must be found. Fortunately, if you are serious about travelling free or cheaply, there are several methods of working a passage by land, sea or air.

SEA

COMMERCIAL SHIPPING

Only registered seafarers are allowed to work on British-registered ships. The only realistic hope for casual employment and attendant transport lies with the more far-flung lines of Scandinavia and the Far East, or with the numerous ships sailing under flags of convenience e.g. Panama, Liberia and the great maritime nation of Liechtenstein. A high percentage of UK ships are flagged out (i.e. registered abroad) to avoid the high cost of unionised British labour. Very occasionally a medium-sized cargo ship takes on an individual with a skill such as catering or carpentry who has petitioned the captain for work, though in the vast majority of cases, merchant ships are fully staffed with low paid, non-unionised workers, many of whom are recruited from Third World countries.

We have heard of very few intrepid travellers who have succeeded with this method. After spending six months in India some years ago, one such traveller went down to the enormous bustling harbour of Bombay (now Mumbai) and asked the captain of a cargo boat from Ghana to take him on as an assistant; within an hour of asking he had set sail for Egypt. His duties were simply to run messages, keep watch and share the cooking duties. More recently Danny Jacobson and his girlfriend found themselves with an idle afternoon in Bangkok:

> Marion and I caught a bus towards the port of Bangkok for a chance of a possible ocean journey to Japan aboard a cargo ship. After an open-windowed ride and a large wander on foot we found ourselves at the wide-open gates of the Royal Port Authority of Bangkok where the great tankers and cargo ships put in to drop and get loads. Cranes and tracks and trucks, the smell of a murky sea and the gray tint of a history of work. Several of those immensely large ships that crash and smash and traverse the mightiest of waves, and/or burn and sink to the Ocean floor, were parked along the concrete bank. A picture of a place one would imagine to be wholly off-limits to pedestrians and tourists yet we walked right past the guard office. Strolling along, admiring the ships, I mentioned how awesome it would be to go aboard and have a look around one, contemplating what it would be like to hitch a ride on a cargo ship. Marion called up to a couple of uniformed guys leaning on the railing of the deck of a nearby ship. 'Hey can we come up?' and they nodded back. We were greeted by a young man from the Philippines who introduced us to the Captain and crew members as though we were important guests. The whole crew was from the Philippines, as was the ship, and they were in Bangkok for a few days before sailing for Japan. Amid idle chat we dropped the idea of us going along to Japan with them. 'Yes, you should come with us,' he said, with an effort towards

the end of the sentence to disqualify the offer. We were not too motivated to push the idea. Anyway, he shifted around the question a bit – have to ask the captain...no room... Soon after he escorted us back down to the deck and we thanked him for the tour.

The harbour authorities can be helpful, especially in countries off the beaten track. (Be careful not to confuse them with customs officers.) They will sometimes show enquirers a list of all the ships arriving and departing, since commercial shipping is almost as carefully regulated as air traffic. Sometimes you will have to ask their permission to go on to the docks, for example in Port Sudan you need to get a permit from the wharf police before you can ask captains for a lift to Mombasa or India. It is worth getting on the right side of the harbour-master since captains may tell him about their need of extra crew. At least, they can advise you about the tides. When it is coming up to high tide (spring tide) boats leave, and so this is a good time to ask around.

CRUISE LINERS

The luxury cruise liner business is absolutely booming. More British holiday-makers go on cruises than take skiing holidays, despite some bad publicity around frequent outbreaks of Norovirus on even the most upmarket cruise ships. Over a thousand liners sail the world's oceans at present, with more being built all the time. These megaliners or resort ships operate on a vast scale, like floating cities, and require a full range of staff. An estimated 15 million people will take a cruise in 2008, an astonishing statistic. Most recruitment takes place through agents or 'concessionaires', all of whom say that they are looking only for qualified and experienced staff. But in many cases it is sufficient to be over 21 and have an extrovert personality and plenty of stamina for the very long hours of work on board.

Jobseekers with no experience or specialised skills should be wary of agencies that invite them to pay a fee to circulate their CV online; this may well work for the highly qualified but there are probably far more people looking for work than there are employers looking for staff this way. Websites to try are: Sea Cruise Enterprises (www.seacruiseent.com) and Ocean Crews Maritime Employment (www.maritimeemployment.com). The privately run site www.cruisejunkie.com includes a link to a no-frills page of cruise-related resources, which includes lists of cruise lines and concessionaires. Another useful list of links can be found in the Cruise Lines section of www.jobmonkey.com (which requires a subscription of $12.95 a month). Many cruise lines have special recruitment sites or pages which will set out how you should apply, e.g. Disney's site www.dcljobs.com has information about its concessionaires worldwide or you can ring the dedicated jobline (407-566-SHIP). For the giant Royal Caribbean, which carries about a quarter of all cruise passengers, go to http://royalcaribbean.hire.com/index.htm; for Radisson Seven Seas Cruises log on to www.rssc.com/employment and for Princess Cruises, check out http://employment.princess.com/employment/index.html).

According to Jane Roberts, who crossed the Atlantic from Venezuela to Estonia as a cruise line croupier, not all employees are experienced professionals:

I worked in the casino department of four different cruise ships and met many people doing jobs as waiters, bar tenders, stewards and stewardesses. These jobs are very easy to come by. In fact 80% of all crew members are people who have never done that particular job in their lives. The turn-over of staff is high, even when people sign year-long contracts, since few people complete them. It is difficult to live and work with the same people 24 hours a day. Crew don't get days off, perhaps just the odd breakfast or lunch off